Why is Everybody Always Picking on Us?

Why is Everybody Always Picking on Us?

Understanding the Roots
of Prejudice

Terrence Webster-Doyle

Illustrations by Rod Cameron

Weatherhill

Published by Weatherhill, Inc.
41 Monroe Turnpike
Trumbull, CT 06611

Copyright © 2000 by Terrence Webster-Doyle

First edition, 2000

Illustrations: Rod Cameron
Editor: Adryan Russ
Creative Consultant: Jean Webster-Doyle

Library of Congress Cataloging-in-Publication Data Available

**A special thanks to
Jean Webster Doyle, my wife, for all your help
in making this book possible.**

**Thank you Christina Clay, my other mother,
who said "Just do it!"**

**Thank you to all of you
who contributed to making it a reality.**

You've Got To Be Carefully Taught

You've got to be taught to hate and fear,
You've got to be taught from year to year,
It's got to be drummed in your dear little ear,
You've got to be carefully taught.

You've got to be taught to be afraid
Of people whose eyes are oddly made
And people whose skin is a different shade,
You've got to be carefully taught.

You've got to be taught before it's too late
Before you are six or seven or eight
To hate all the people your relatives hate
You've got to be carefully taught . . .
You've got to be carefully taught.

—From *South Pacific*
© 1949 Lyrics by Oscar Hammerstein II
Music by Richard Rogers

Life Is Full of Challenges

You've already learned how to do many complicated things in your life— walk, talk, ride a bicycle, do math, use a computer. Now that you know how to do them, they don't seem difficult. Learning about prejudice is like that. Little by little, you can learn what it is, why it exists, and what you can do to prevent it.

Although some of the words and ideas you read in this book may be new to you, with practice and a little help from a caring adult, you'll be able to understand them all. All you need is a desire to learn. It's up to you.

So, as you read, bear this thought in mind:

We have created prejudice with uneducated thinking.
We can undo it with intelligent understanding.

Life is full of challenges. Each of us can meet and overcome them. This book will give you the confidence and skills to do that.

Are you interested in facing the challenges? Are you ready to be tested? Let's find out. And as you face these new challenges, remember that you are not alone. We can do it together.

Table of Contents

Introduction

What is prejudice?

Has anyone ever called you a name you hate?

What does this name make you feel when you hear it?

If you've been called a name you don't like by people who know
   you don't like it . . . you've been a victim of bullying!

This is a result of prejudice.

WARNING
Prejudice and bullying can cause your brain
to get you to act in ways that hurt people—
even without your knowing it!

The only way we can deal with the truth is to meet it face-to-face.

Where did prejudice start?

How can it be stopped?

Keep reading and find out.

Prejudice Begins at an Early Age

The book you are about to read is about prejudice, about people picking on and bullying other people—usually only because those people seem "different." Prejudice that causes bullying starts at a very young age. Children learn to fear and hate others because they are taught to do so. They are "programmed" over a period of time to believe that certain people are dangerous, lazy, stupid, strange—or for some other reason not worthy of our respect. After a while, these ideas become part of their view of life—a view based on prejudice. Consider:

Little children have no prejudices.
Their minds are free.
They don't see differences between people.

Why do you think this is? I think it's because babies are innocent—naturally free of mental images and feelings that cause conflict between themselves and others. But after a time, they start to learn about differences and to fear them.

I think it is important, right from the start, to tell you that no one is to blame. When we blame someone, we believe that the person is wrong, or bad. I think that blame only causes pain, because it can create hate. If someone has been taught to be prejudiced, it's not his or her fault. It just happens. It's automatic, like when the doctor taps your knee with a rubber hammer, causing it to jump.

I think that people who become prejudiced don't *understand* what has happened to them. They aren't *aware* of what they are thinking or doing.

10

When we're young, we're impressionable. This means that we can be easily persuaded to do things we may not really want to do. Have you ever been coaxed into doing something you didn't want to do? Well, then you understand. This is how we can get mixed up. We don't start out that way, but what we learn from others can sometimes confuse us as we grow up.

But there is a time when we *must* understand what we're doing and take responsibility for our prejudice. That's what this book is about. When people become *aware* of the prejudice that's been programmed into their brains, they can be free of it.

Blame and hate prevent understanding.
So instead of blaming or hating people for what they do, can we learn to understand *why* we bully, *why* we act in prejudiced ways?

I know first-hand what it feels like to be bullied. I was a big kid who was picked on a lot. I had feelings of rage and frustration, and they caused me terrible pain. I'm hoping that you won't have to go through that pain.

Have you ever felt teased, taunted, put down, embarrassed, or picked on, because you were "different"? If you have, you've been a victim of prejudice, and hopefully this book can help you. It will show you what prejudice is, where it comes from, what effects it has on people, and what you can do to end it, right where it starts—at its roots.

Take this journey with me—to the roots of prejudice—and together we'll discover how we can be free of it.

A Journey to the Roots

Do you believe that you have no prejudices? Would you be surprised to learn that you do?

If you discovered that you do have prejudices, would you want to keep them? Change them? Talk about them?

Are you aware that many of the habits you pick up come from family, friends, radio, television, the movies—things you read, stories you were told, and rules you've been taught?

Have you ever questioned things you see and hear? Have you listened to other people's opinions and then made a decision to act based on your own thinking?

Have you ever looked for the "roots" of the prejudice you've witnessed?

Often students will say to me, "I don't understand what you mean by the *roots* of prejudice. I can see prejudice when someone hates someone because the other person is different. But I don't see what you call *the roots.*"

So, I take them out and we sit under a tree together and talk.

I say, "Look at the tree we're sitting under. See how many leaves there are? The leaves grow on branches, and the branches sprout from limbs, and the limbs are all attached to the trunk of the tree. Now follow the trunk of the tree as far down as you can. See below the ground?"

"Roots!" they say.

"Exactly!" I tell them. "The roots come out of a seed, which is where the tree begins its life. Without roots, there would be no trunk, no limbs, no branches, no leaves.

"That's how it is with prejudice. If it had no roots, there would be no hatred, no conflict, no feelings of superiority or inferiority."

"No prejudice!" they say.

"Yes," I tell them. "Like the leaves of a tree, all prejudices—no matter how different they seem—all share one root—one basic cause. If we're going to find out what causes prejudice, we have to find its roots. Like archaeologists who search for objects from ancient civilizations, we can make our own discoveries. We can uncover what prejudice is, how it grows, and how it spreads. Together we can explore prejudices we've lived with all our lives, and take a hard look at how these "programmed" reactions work today in our own lives.

The best way to think for ourselves is to ask questions, and it's important to think carefully before responding to any question. We need to search our thoughts the way a computer searches every file when it is trying to find a particular document. On such a search, there are no "right" or "wrong" answers—only honest ones. On such a journey, we can make some amazing discoveries.

DISCOVERY 1
When you can observe clearly for yourself, you can stop prejudice.

Millions upon millions of people have suffered and died because of prejudice, all because they didn't understand it. People today talk about "tolerating" it, but tolerating means allowing it to exist. In today's world, we allow prejudice to exist.

To put an end to prejudice, we must understand what *creates* it, at its roots, in *ourselves*. That means, besides looking at what others say and do, we have to look at the way we think and the way we act.

Where to Look

Prejudice is definitely something that can end. But in order for it to do so, we need to know where to start—where to look. We're all aware of its symptoms—sorrow, anger and fear. But in order to end it *before* hurtful feelings begin—we need to see its causes, right when they're starting. Then, we can nip them in the bud.

Have you ever had a terrible toothache? The dentist may have to remove a rotten tooth. But removing a tooth won't help prevent a future toothache in another tooth. To prevent tooth decay, you need to understand the *cause* of tooth decay — what you, yourself, do to create it. Maybe you eat too much sugar. Maybe you don't brush your teeth after meals. Maybe you don't floss.

Prejudice is like tooth decay.
It starts deep inside.
Once we see a symptom, the decay has already begun.

Have you heard of preventive dentistry? Its goal is to stop decay *before* it gets to the surface. So, to practice preventive prejudice, we must stop hate *before* it gets to the surface. When people act hatefully toward each other, it's too late. If we can get to conflict between people *before* it happens—at the beginning, right where the prejudice starts—we can prevent it from happening.

The Four Stages of Learning

Our journey of discovery in this book will consist of four stages to help us understand how prejudice works. We will begin by simply *thinking* about prejudice—what it means, when it has happened, and how it affected you or someone you know. Then we will actually *observe* it as it happens in the moment, right now! And we'll talk about what we see.

If we stay in the conceptual stage, where we only *think* about prejudice, we'll understand the words. But *experience* of prejudice comes when we perceive it—when we see it as it's happening.

Talking about prejudice is important. It not only helps us learn, but it helps relieve any fears we have about it. And history has shown us that people who remain silent—people who do not talk about it—tend to be those who suffer the most. Again, the Four Stages of Learning are:

Stage 1. *Think* about prejudice and what it generally means.

Stage 2. *Remember* how prejudice has personally affected you or people you know.

Stage 3. *Observe* prejudice as it happens in your brain. This awareness is called "insight."

Stage 4. *Talk* with another person about the prejudice you observe.

To help us get started, let's use these four stages to understand something very simple, for example, an orange.

Stage 1. *Think.* I tell you how an orange looks, feels and tastes, giving you a general description of an orange. You *think* about it and try to *visualize* it in your mind.

Stage 2. *Remember.* You tell me that you *recognize* what an orange is, because you've eaten one and you know other people who have eaten and enjoyed oranges.

Stage 3. *Observe.* I give you an *actual* orange so that you can see it, feel it and taste it first-hand. You actually perceive it—not in your mind, but live, in person.

Stage 4. *Discuss.* You tell someone about the orange, not from just imagining it, but from personally tasting it, based on your own *experience,* your own *observation.*

Suppose someone lived at the North Pole, with no chance to see or taste an orange. He or she would have to *imagine* what an orange really is, based on someone else's description. But at some point, to really understand what an orange is, that person will have to actually *observe and experience the orange personally.* And that's how it is with prejudice.

DISCOVERY 2
**The best way to understand the meaning of prejudice
is to experience it firsthand.**

The Journey Begins

In prehistoric time, the only focus of every single day was survival—nothing but survival. Can you imagine it? You may be amazed to learn that human beings at that time had needs very similar to yours.

Let's return to the beginning of human evolution. Let's go back in time to when there were no modern homes, no tall buildings, no stores, no automobiles—only blue sky, miles and miles of open land, and simple, primitive human beings. Then, perhaps we'll discover where prejudice really began.

WHAT IS PREJUDICE?

Chapter One
Where Prejudice Began

The Roots of Prejudice

The night was black, and the jungle came alive with the sound of hooting owls, howling wolves, and the crackling of branches breaking under the stealthy steps of hungry saber-toothed tigers. Several humans were huddled together in silence inside a bare, cliffside cave. The sun had fallen and the sliver of a moon was their only light. Dark clouds hid the stars.

The people knew that the night meant danger. They were aware that the purpose of every nighttime gathering in the cave was simply to survive the darkness and live through the long wait for the first sign of morning light. Being with the group made each of them feel more secure. They knew that if they wound up alone after nightfall, they might be helpless against the attack of a larger animal.

"Hoot!" "Growl!" "Squawk!" They jumped and turned their heads toward where the sounds appeared to be coming from. Pressed close together, their ears were sharply attuned to every sound, and their eyes scanned the darkness slowly and carefully. As tired as they were, they knew that falling asleep was risky. But since they were gathered together, they felt safer. They took turns watching the children and taking short naps.

At last dawn was breaking, signaling their survival of another night. As the sun came up, they felt relieved. Their thoughts now turned to what they had to accomplish to survive the day. They shared the labors. One woman cooked food that had been gathered the day before while another tidied up. The older children cared for the smaller ones. The men hunted and brought back food. Each member of the group had a job to do; each relied on the others. Their very lives depended on everyone contributing to the whole.

The Rock Tribe

In their own language, they called themselves the Rock Tribe, because everywhere they looked, they could see rocks. There were many children now in the tribe, and it was becoming more difficult to keep track of them. To keep the tribe together, the older people—the elders—created activities to be performed by tribe members of the group. One of these was that each person would create a pile of rocks, which the tribe would worship. The elders were superstitious. They believed the rocks represented the mysterious forces of nature and that if the tribe did not worship these forces, it would perish.

The elders determined that, every month, everyone in the Rock Tribe would dance to the rising sun to frighten away evil spirits. They further specified that all tribe members must paint their faces with a specific design to show that they all belonged to the Rock Tribe. The patterns drawn on their faces ensured that members would recognize their own.

Over time these activities were carried out again and again—so often that they became customs, ritual practices the tribe carried out on a regular basis. They would paint their faces even if they were exhausted from the day's work. They would dance to the sun even if it rained or snowed. These recurring practices gave them a sense of belonging.

The group members became so accustomed to their repetitious ways of life, that painting their faces and dancing to the sun soon became habit—something they did without thinking. Once a month, when the sun arose, they painted their faces and danced. And so it was, month after month, year after year.

From Habit to Patriotism

These customs were passed from one generation to the next, by the elders to their children, and then those children became elders and passed these customs down to *their* children. In so doing, these **beliefs** became firmly ingrained in the minds and hearts of tribe members—beliefs held so closely that they became **traditions.** Everyone would sit around a fire at night, and the elders would describe the traditions that had come down from their ancestors. Storytelling kept the beliefs and traditions alive.

One day, something different happened. As usual, the cry came as the sun arose and the sky lightened: "Time to dance to the sun!" But for the first time, a tribe member refused to do what the others were doing.

"Yako is not dancing to the sun! He must be punished!" cried one of the elders. And so the young member of the Rock Tribe was made to stay home, to not hunt with the others, and to live on nothing but water for three days.

The repeated practice had become a **custom,** and the custom had become a **tradition.** These unquestioned traditions became the foundation of the tribe's heritage—rules they lived by and, as a result, became **law.** These specific ancestral regulations defined their ways, the rules by which this particular tribe's descendants were to live. They considered these rules to be their **tribal inheritance**—their **birthright**—something of value to honor forever. This was a **legacy** they could leave to their children and their children's children.

And so they went on. No one stopped to ask *why* they continued to perform these practices and live by these laws. Their thinking had become "conditioned." They were "programmed" to think and act in a certain way. And so they did.

The tribe's beliefs and traditions became a part of their culture, which, as their population and territory grew, identified them as a nation. The nation developed pride and honor, which caused a feeling of patriotism in all tribe members.

This path from ritual to nation to patriotism bonded the tribe members for centuries, carrying the past into the present. And what this provided tribe members was something they valued more than anything: survival!

The Drive to Survive

When the world seemed a larger place and there were far fewer people than today, small groups of people formed tribes and engaged in ritual practices which, performed for thousands of years, made them feel secure. Living with many people made them feel safe.

Today, we still live in small groups like tribes, not the kind that our ancestors experienced, but like tribes nevertheless. We live within families and belong to clubs, organizations, houses of worship, or political parties. All of these groups help establish our identity, our sense of who we are, although, unlike in the past, we do not rely on them for our safety,

In fact, since the world today has become a smaller place, and people from *all over the world* must depend on each other for survival, the old ways of individual tribes, as well as those of our modern groups, no longer help make us safe. Instead, they can divide us and even prevent us from contributing to the welfare of one another, as one race—the human race.

DISCOVERY 3
In modern times, tribal groups and tribe-like behavior can threaten the security of our human race. Why? Because they separate people.

What Does It Mean to Survive?

Ancient tribal people bonded as a group because they were afraid that if they didn't belong to a group, they could not survive. What do you think they specifically feared? Let's explore this. There are two kinds of survival—**physical** and **psychological**.

We survive **physically** when we have enough to eat and drink, clothes to keep us warm and a place to live. An ancient tribe, or clan, helped its members survive physically by giving them physical security—guaranteeing them food, clothing, shelter and protection.

We survive **psychologically** when we feel safe and secure. Each ancient tribe member was required to "identify" with the group by following the group's customs and beliefs. Members had to attach themselves *mentally* and *emotionally* to the group and loyally follow its ways. Such a following made the group more powerful, and thus better able to take care of its members.

DISCOVERY 4
food + shelter = physical needs
sharing a way of life with others = psychological needs
physical needs + psychological needs = safety and security

A sense of safety and security comes when both our physical and mental needs are satisfied.

Growth: A New Threat to Survival

With their physical and psychological needs met, an ancient tribe felt safe. Over time, however, individual tribes began to grow bigger, so big that their territories bumped against the territories of other groups. Since all of the tribes needed food, clothing, and shelter, each began to see every other tribe as a threat to its physical survival.

22

And, since the psychological survival of the tribes was tied to their physical needs, they believed that their customs, traditions, and beliefs were also threatened. This created conflict between the tribes, which led to war, not only over territory and physical needs, but also over whose beliefs should dominate, whose birthright should rule, and whose laws should govern in order to ensure everyone's survival.

Are Tools and Technology Enough to Survive?

Challenged by the problems of physical survival, science eventually developed remarkable tools and technology that gave us the ability to create more easily the food, clothing, and shelter we need. While there were people who didn't have a place to live or enough food to eat—and we still face that problem today—we know far more about creating *physical* elements of survival than we ever had before.

Yet, *psychological* conflict continued. Science seemed to have no way to resolve the different ideas people had about "how life should be." You can imagine, for example, a member of a different tribe saying, "The Rock Tribe dances when the sun rise! They really *ought to* dance to the moon, as we do!" Each tribe believed that their customs and traditions were correct, and necessary to ensure their survival. Each feared doing things in a different way.

The need to protect their traditions, to ensure their psychological survival, prevented tribes from cooperating at the physical level. As a result, many groups remained in conflict with other groups. And the reason for their conflict was fear.

DISCOVERY 5
Fear creates conflict.

The Birth of Prejudice

As time passed, ideas of how to live still separated people into groups similar to tribes. Even though scientific discovery had taught them how to feed and clothe themselves, people were still *psychologically* attached to their groups. This attachment caused members of a group to see everything around them in a particular, opinionated way.

Somebody would say, "Those people go to that club on the corner! They really *should* belong to ours!"

The word "should," like the phrase "ought to," implies that one person knows better than the other person. This kind of divisive thinking separated groups from one another and caused conflict between them. The conflict caused feelings of prejudice.

They would say, for example, "We cannot speak to people who believe that religion! Their thoughts are certainly *of lesser value* than ours!"

And so the people continued their old tribal ways through the ages. The prejudices they felt were passed down, generation after generation, until you and I were born.

Now *our* brains are the ones that are conditioned. And the question is: Do we want to keep passing these prejudices of our "Forgotten Ancestors" into the future? Do we want to continue to be prisoners of the past?

DISCOVERY 6
Deeply ingrained in our brain cells, old tribal ways continue to make us prisoners of the past.

A World Without Prejudice

Can we imagine a world where people are *not* conditioned to react to other people? What would that be like? What if we studied how ancient tribes couldn't get together because they all had become prejudiced by the customs, traditions, and beliefs that had been conditioned into them by their Forgotten Ancestors? And what if we decided, as a result of studying their methods and customs, that we didn't want to be that way?

This new world would inspire students to understand prejudice and how it comes about. Classes would be offered in which students and teachers could create projects to uncover how prejudice works.

The new world would create a new generation of students who would shake themselves free from the shadows of their Forgotten Ancestors, free from conditioned thinking and established beliefs of the past. The new world would graduate students who become Peace Ambassadors and help educate people about new insights they had acquired. These students would become Citizens of the World and make an exciting discovery about tribal identity.

DISCOVERY 7
Our survival depends upon understanding we are all members of one tribe—the Human Race.

Students would no longer need to think like the members of any particular group. While they might still participate in some group activities, they no longer would believe that mental and emotional security comes from belonging to a group. They no longer would need to belong to a tribe-like club to find out how to think and act. Old opinions and beliefs that had once prevented them from thinking and acting in peaceful ways would fade, and the differences that had kept them apart from one another would fall away.

The new world would be a place where prejudices, inherited traditions, and customs were no longer needed for protection. The only need would be that of the good of all humankind.

The Human Rainbow

Students of this new world would learn to appreciate cultural *differences*—in such areas as architecture, food, clothing, and language. These variations wouldn't divide them or create prejudice, but interest them and enrich them, creating a world of diversity and variety. They would learn that:

- Cultural *conditioning* creates division; division creates conflict; conflict causes suffering.
- People can be "different," yet be of one race.
- The human race consists of unique individuals, yet it is one.
- Human diversity is a rainbow of complementary colors.
- Cultural *variety* enhances life and gives great pleasure.

DISCOVERY 8
You can change the world when you think for yourself.
A journey of a thousand miles begins with the first step.

IN-SIGHTS

★ The very first people on earth created practices for group members to perform. Creating these activities made them all feel closer and safer.

★ Their practices became customs; their customs became traditions and laws; their tribes became nations with different cultures. Over time, members accepted the beliefs without questioning.

★ Tribal members have bonded for centuries, because they've been convinced that their beliefs and laws helped them survive.

★ Today, we still live among tribe-like groups—families, companies, communities, clubs, houses of worship, cities, counties, and nations. As this new millennium begins, there are billions of people around the world, and we are all dependent upon one another for survival.

★ Today, groups who believe other people "should" and "ought to" act according to their established beliefs, without question, can separate people and create conflict. They can even be a threat to the security and survival of the human race.

★ There are two kinds of survival—physical and psychological. We survive physically by having enough to eat and drink, clothes to keep us warm and a place to live. We survive psychologically by feeling secure. When both our physical and psychological needs are satisfied, we feel safe.

★ Despite the development of tools and technology that provide physical comforts, psychological conflict continues.

★ Because we've all inherited some of the old tribal ways from our ancestors, their prejudice is still alive in all of us—in the ways we've been conditioned to think and act.

★ Our greatest goal is to understand ourselves and how we relate to other people, and to recognize how we create conflict—in ourselves and in the world.

THINKING FOR YOURSELF

◆ Can you describe the relationship between a practice and a custom? Between a tradition and a law? A culture and a nation? A nation and patriotism?

◆ Does it seem to you that each of these—practice, custom, tradition, law—tends to blend into the next, while growing bigger and stronger? Why do you think that happens?

◆ What is an example of a habit you have? What is a custom you perform regularly? If you attend religious serves, what is a repeated practice you do there? Do you belong to an organization that has rules?

◆ What is a tradition practiced by you or your family? Do you celebrate certain holidays? Eat certain foods at certain times?

◆ What beliefs do you have about life? What do you think is your heritage or birthright?

◆ What tribe-like groups do you know about? Which ones do you belong to?

Family	Club	Organization
Cultural center	Company	Political group
City or State	Ethnic Group	Nation

◆ Is the "tribe" you belong to different from other "tribes" you know? If so, how?

◆ Do you think belonging to such "tribes" enhances your safety? Do you think that belonging to a group affects the way you see the world? How?

◆ Do you think we need to fight today in order to survive? In order to have true peace will we need to give up *identifying* with our individual tribes or groups? Why?

◆ Can we have a world in which our differences do not create conflict? A world in which we can take pleasure in our diversity?

Chapter Two
What We're Taught To Believe

The Highest Level of Understanding

Learning about prejudice can be disturbing. When we read news reports of devastating clashes between cultures, nations, and races, we become painfully aware of how badly some people have been treated because of their color, their upbringing, or their beliefs. But if we study these reports with the intent to learn how prejudice works, perhaps we can reach a level of understanding that will help us *see* where prejudice begins—at its roots.

A good way to begin is to use our scientific minds. One chief purpose of scientific thought is to allow us to make correct predictions about events. The reason for this is that we—just like our prehistoric ancestors—want to survive. Scientists want to be able to predict the next earthquake, tornado, or hurricane so that we can protect ourselves from those disasters and survive. That's why we listen to weather reports, traffic reports, and news broadcasts about what's happening in the world.

So, if we treat the study of prejudice as a science project, we can get better at surviving in another way. We can learn how to protect ourselves from ignorance, fear, and the day-to-day pressure brought about by our conditioned way of looking at the world. Just like exploring how a car engine works, how a flower grows, or how to produce cleaner air, examining prejudice teaches us to survive by using the highest level of understanding—by learning how to get along with people.

What Does Prejudice Mean?

If you throw a punch at someone and hurt him, there's a good chance you're going to hurt your hand, too. Prejudice is like that. It hurts everyone—not only the person being bullied, but the bully, too.

Sometimes we don't think before we act. There are times we are given information that simply is not true and, more often than not, we don't stop to question it. The first step in becoming free of prejudice is learning to question everything

we hear and see. We'll be doing a lot of that. So, let "Who?" "What?" "Where?" "How?" and "Why?" become your favorite words as our journey continues.

The act of prejudice is not based on fact, it's based on *judgment*. (Are you already asking why?) Many times we believe we are stating a fact, when, in reality, we are only repeating what we have heard, making an assumption, or expressing an opinion.

DEFINITION 1
Prejudice is judging, assuming, or expressing our opinion *before* we have all the right information.

If I were to ask you, "What do you think of vanilla ice cream?" you might say, "It's my favorite!" Or, "Too bland! I prefer chocolate!" Your opinion about vanilla ice cream would be based on the fact that you've tasted it, and you know whether or not you like that particular flavor. You've had *firsthand experience* with that ice cream.

If I asked you, "What do you think of the artist Pablo Picasso?" you might say, "He's terrific!" Or, "Too abstract for me!" Or, "I don't know—I've never seen his work." Your opinion would be based on whether or not you've *seen* Picasso's work. If you haven't had firsthand experience with this artist's work, it would be difficult to express an honest opinion.

Now, here's a case that's a bit different. I could ask you, "What do you think of that new student who just came here from the Ukraine?"

You might say, "He seems pretty stupid! Every time I say something to him, he just smiles."

Would your opinion be based on fact? Firsthand information? Someone else's opinion? In this case, none of those would be true! In fact, your opinion would be a definite sign of prejudice. Can you guess why?

The reason is that you've decided someone is "stupid" based on no real evidence. You've *assumed* a lack of intelligence without knowing whether the person is stupid or smart! If you haven't been able to talk to him, how do you really know? Maybe he doesn't speak English very well. Is it fair to judge him as stupid just because his native language is not the same as yours? How would you like it if you were visiting a foreign country—perhaps China or Hungary— and every one you met assumed that *you* were stupid, because you couldn't speak *their* language?

So, now we know that one kind of prejudice is judging before we have all the right information. Another kind of prejudice happens when we judge people because we don't understand their thoughts or actions.

DEFINITION 2
**To be prejudiced is to judge a person or group
simply because they act or appear different from us.**

What could possibly make us hate someone we've never met? And why would we automatically hate people just because they're different? If I told you that there's a new student in school who discovered that you were not born in this country, and she hates you because of it—how would you feel? In a way, it's like sending an innocent person to jail. The person has to suffer, but has no idea why.

Like a weed that multiplies, prejudice pops up, seemingly out of nowhere, and spreads like wildfire. Can you think of a time someone called you names or tried to bully or hurt you—simply because you were different? If so, for a long time after, you may have felt angry and strongly prejudiced against the person who bullied you. That person, who acted in a prejudiced way toward you, has triggered feelings of prejudice inside you, and now you feel prejudiced toward him or her.

See how prejudice can grow? Even though that incident is long gone, you keep remembering it, and reliving it.

DISCOVERY 9
**Although prejudice may be something you encountered in the past,
it can continue, and make you unhappy in the present.**

What Does It Mean to Be Different?

As we have seen, the roots of prejudice began with the formation of groups, or tribes. Each tribe was forced to protect its territory and its ways. Any individual outside the tribe was discriminated against for being different. But tribe members *within* a tribe also had to deal with prejudice. Since each individual had to obey tribal rules, any attempt to be different was punished.

31

All over the world, little conflicts go on every day. Maybe someone has called you names or tried to bully you because you were different. It happened to me, and I still feel the pain of it—not physically, but inside, in my feelings and memory.

But what's wrong with different? If I told you there was a new theme park in town, and that it had an amazing ride, something different from anything you'd ever been on before, would you instantly hate it? Probably not. Would you want to go there and try the ride? Probably so. In this case, different means exciting and new. Or how about if I told you there's a new candy bar so different from anything you've ever tasted, you'd never want to eat any other candy bar again? Wouldn't it interest you— even if it's different?

With the possibility of such exciting and tempting characteristics, what would make something different unappealing? Why would someone who dresses differently, or speaks differently, or thinks differently be less exciting than a new ride or a delicious new candy bar? Do you think some kind of prejudice is at work here?

Prejudice can lead to an irrational attitude of hostility directed toward an individual or group. What this means is that you and I can be taught to think in ways that make us dislike, or even hate, another person without ever understanding why—without understanding how we could be taught to think and act this way.

Anything that can slip inside us, fester and grow like a weed, without our being aware of it, is troubling. But we can do something about it. Can you and I look upon other people's customs and traditions without judging them? Is it possible for us to develop an understanding about life that ends prejudice?

We think there is, and as you continue reading, we'll discover it together.

IN-SIGHTS

★ An important purpose of scientific thought is to make correct predictions about natural events; the reason for this is we want to ensure our survival.

★ Examining prejudice teaches us to survive using the highest level of intelligence—by learning how to get along with other people.

★ Prejudice is something that prevents us from getting along with other people.

★ Prejudice means to dislike someone only because he or she seems different.

★ An act of prejudice is not based on fact, but on an opinion that is often formed without real reason or sufficient knowledge.

★ As scientists, we need to ask: Is what we believe a fact, or an opinion? Do we have firsthand information, or are we simply assuming something?

★ Feelings of hatred between people have caused tremendous suffering and pain to many generations over thousands of years.

★ When we explore the roots of prejudice in ourselves and in others, we get better at surviving fear, ignorance and day-to-day pressures.

★ Continuing to be angry about something that happened in the past only sustains our unhappiness in the present.

★ Many people throughout history have been punished for being different. But different doesn't imply bad; it could be something new and exciting.

THINKING FOR YOURSELF

◆ Have you ever judged beforehand—made a decision before you had all the information? What were the circumstances?

◆ Have you ever hated someone for being different? How was that person different?

◆ Did you ever pass along a rumor without knowing for certain whether it was true? What was the rumor?

◆ Did the rumor have a positive or negative effect on someone you know?

◆ Do you think any act of prejudice can possibly be based on fact? If so, what is that act?

◆ Can you see how continuing to think about something sad that happened in the past can continue to make you unhappy in the present?

◆ Can you see how a prejudiced thought, constantly alive in your brain, can continue the prejudice instead of allowing it to go away?

◆ Why do you think scientists want to make correct predictions about nature? Is this another human attempt to make sure we survive?

◆ How do you think examining the roots of prejudice can help us survive?

◆ How can examining the roots of prejudice help us protect ourselves from fear, ignorance, and stressful situations that we encounter every day?

Chapter Three
Our Mechanical Brains

Do We Protect Ourselves, or Do We Learn?

When we hear about or read a news story that is shocking, a natural reaction is to want to push it away, forget about it, to protect ourselves from even thinking about something so horrible. But is it really better to protect ourselves, or is it better to learn?

Prejudice is a way of thinking that usually leads us to negative judgments. For this reason, it is usually described as something bad—something we should protect ourselves from and something we "should not do." But if we're going to be scientists, it's important for us to remain fair and impartial when we are exploring any subject we decide to study. If we decide that something is bad before we've even begun to study it—then *we* are the ones being prejudiced. Learning about prejudice requires a mind that looks factually, without judgment, at the root causes of prejudice. Why? So that we may understand how it happens.

Sometimes it's difficult to look because of the suffering prejudice has generated. Perhaps you've already experienced this kind of pain. Perhaps some people have perceived you as different and, as a result, have picked on you or bullied you. If you've felt the pain of prejudiced attitudes and words, you already have a good reason to want prejudice to end. Whatever your reason, learning to understand it will help you end it—before it even begins. And hopefully this understanding will help you avoid conflict and prevent future conflicts.

We Have a Mechanical Brain

When your TV screen shows nothing but jagged, diagonal lines, you know there's something wrong with it. Well, prejudice in our thinking acts just like that. It's like a machine in our head programs us to act in ways that are hurtful, ways that create static and conflict. Prejudice is a mechanical problem.

Our Mechanical Brains

For example, let's say someone tells you that someone you know is a bad person, perhaps because of his or her race, cultural beliefs, or nationality. This thought is programmed into your thinking, creating a "groove" there, and becoming ingrained in your thought processes. This often happens in three stages:

1. When a message first enters your brain, you get an image in your mind.
   John says Jan is bad.
2. As the message is repeated, the image is reinforced.
   John said Jan is bad.
   Now Alice says Jan is dishonest, and Patrick says Jan is mean.
3. The image causes a negative feeling to develop.
   I hate Jan, because she is a bad, dishonest, mean person.

Messages + Repetition = Image + Feeling

Are these words about Jan true? Are they based on fact? You don't really know. They're only the opinions of others. Still, they create an image through constant repetition, an image that is false because it is based on messages that are not known to be true.

Regardless of its truth, however, that image in turn creates a feeling. So one day you see Jan and the image and feeling pop up in your head, like when a doctor taps your knee with a hard rubber mallet and your knee jerks. It's mechanical, automatic—it happens unconsciously, without your being aware of it. You can't control it. The image and feeling are programmed in the brain and triggered when you see Jan. Then they are projected outward—like a movie projector projects an image onto a screen. But the image you're projecting is in your brain—it isn't real!

DISCOVERY 10
Prejudice is like a House of Mirrors.
All the images you have of others are created by you.

You think that what you see is actually happening in the real world outside yourself. But it's not! It's happening in only one place—your head! And so you move on, believing that what your brain has told you is factual but, in reality, you've been judging. And by judging, you have not been understanding!

The Scientific Method for Understanding

Understanding is one of the chief goals of a scientist. So, in order to continue our exploration of how prejudice works, we must do everything in our power to use our minds according to a scientific method that promotes understanding. Here are some simple rules:

Remain cool and calm.
Examine the subject thoroughly.
Question without assuming.
Test findings to see whether they are factual.

Remain cool and calm. There's a lot to be said for being able to think and act in an objective way when we find ourselves in an unknown or even frightening situation. Consider the alternative: What are the chances for our understanding a situation if we are so angry that we cannot speak?

ASK YOURSELF
When I'm angry, what's happening?

Examine the subject thoroughly. In order to understand a thing or a person thoroughly, a good scientist must examine him or her or it from every conceivable point of view. When we're upset or in a hurry, we do not take the time to consider every perspective.

ASK YOURSELF
What can I do to make sure that
I look at a situation from all possible viewpoints?

Question without assuming "This must be right" or "That must be wrong." Suppose we have seen a video reporting a conflict going on between two groups in another country. And suppose that I have relatives belonging to one of the groups, while you have relatives that belong to the other. Does this automatically make us enemies? Do we immediately assume the "side" of the group with whom we are connected, regardless of how loosely? Do we question what it means to be identified with a certain group, way of thinking, or way of life?

ASK YOURSELF
Why do I feel that this is right and that is wrong?
Is my judgment based on facts or merely assumptions?

Test findings to see whether they are factual. When you hear a rumor about someone, do you automatically accept it as truth?

ASK YOURSELF
How can I find out the real facts of the situation?

As we continue our study of prejudice, we'll double-check these steps from time to time, to make certain that we continue to follow the scientific method.

Many Prejudices—But One Root

We tend to think of prejudice as something that comes from outside us, but the truth is, it begins *inside* us. While its roots may have been passed to us by people who came before us, the prejudice that now lives and breathes within you and me comes from *within*.

You know how you can be drinking the last gulp of water from a glass, and you look through the glass, and everything you're looking at appears a bit squashed or elongated? These are the shapes of prejudice.

DISCOVERY 11
Prejudice causes our thinking to get "out of focus," making us judge what we see inaccurately.

What this does is create inner conflict. We are at war with ourselves, inside our minds. Seeing something or someone as "bad," "wrong," "stupid," or "different" immediately creates conflict in our minds—between bad and good, right and wrong, ignorant and smart. We start to think, "That person is bad. I am good." Or, "That person is right. I must be wrong." Or, "I'm ignorant, and that bully is smart."

Can we look and see if any of these thoughts are true? Or are they all opinions we've formulated in our minds that have caused us to become prejudiced?

From Within to Without

Once we think and act from prejudice we feel inside, we put our prejudice outside ourselves. We act negatively toward someone we perceive as "bad," and tend to act superior to someone we perceive as "stupid." Over the years, we have created a long list of categories that we can use to distinguish ourselves from others, to dislike others or feel superior to them, including skin color, age, race, nationality or culture, religion, gender, social class, occupation, body size, and physical abilities (and diabilities!).

Such a long list of possible differences easily allows us to separate "us" from "them" and to become "reasons" to treat each other badly. If we look at them carefully, however, we see that they are not anything good or bad, but simply images programmed in the brain—your brain, my brain, everyone's brain. Moreover, they prevent us from thinking about all the ways we are the same. Couldn't we just as easily focus on our similarities? What do we have in common? What do we mutually like?

What A Difference A Word Makes

Look at the following two ways of asking a question. What can you tell about the attitude of the person asking each question?

"Why doesn't the radio work?"
"What moron broke the radio?"

Which question seeks an answer? Which one judges? It's easy to see, isn't it? Read the following two questions. How would you feel if you were John or Philippe?

"Why does John like to hang out with Philippe?"
"Why does that idiot John hang out with that foreigner?

Which one questions? Which one judges? Isn't it amazing how one or two words can stir up an image that creates conflict?

Programmed images are part of the basic structure in our brains, and are triggered by such words as "moron," and "foreigner." And this careless use of such powerful "image-provoking" words can create the worst outcome of prejudice—conflict. When prejudice lives inside us, and we put it outside ourselves and act prejudiced toward another human being, that's exactly what we're doing—we're setting the stage for conflict between ourselves and someone else.

Prejudice Inside Us ▹ Prejudice Outside Us = Conflict

Our brain is capable of great thoughts, but also, unfortunately, false images. Learning to recognize the difference is essential. In the better world we wish to create, is there any reason for any group of people to feel superior to any other group of people?

What do *you* think?

IN-SIGHTS

★ Prejudice is a way of thinking that usually leads us to negative judgments. When we judge something with prejudice, we cannot really understand it.

★ Learning about prejudice requires a mind that looks, without judgment, at the roots or causes of prejudice.

★ Prejudice has caused many people great pain and suffering, and continues to do so.

★ Learning to understand prejudice helps to end it.

★ As scientists, we must ask ourselves: Do I want to learn, or do I want to protect myself from something unpleasant? Do I see people as different, or do I really want to understand them?

★ The scientific method for understanding requires that we:
Remain cool and calm

Examine the subject thoroughly

Question without assuming

Test findings to see whether they are factual

★ Prejudice is like a machine in our heads that programs us to act in ways that are hurtful.

★ The image that prejudice causes our brain to display is created by the repetition of a message, and it lives in only one place—the brain.

★ In the new world we wish to create there is no reason for any person or group to feel superior or inferior to another.

THINKING FOR YOURSELF

◆ Do you think we can understand something if we make assumptions about it? Why?

◆ Has someone else's prejudice ever hurt you? How do you think that person's prejudice began?

◆ Do you understand what it means to have a brain that is "programmed"?

◆ Can you think of an image in your brain of something you have never experienced directly? How did that image get there?

◆ Can you see that the image is created automatically? That it happens unconsciously, without your being aware of it?

◆ Do you know a group of people who believe they are "superior" to others in some way? Why do they? Do you agree with their reasons?

◆ Do you think there is a good reason for any group to feel superior to any other group?

◆ Have you ever felt that people of your skin color were superior to people of another skin color? Have you ever felt that people of another skin color believed themselves superior to you?

◆ Do you think you have a good reason to feel superior to someone else? Do you think anyone has good reason to feel superior to you? Explain why you think so.

◆ Has someone else's prejudice ever hurt you? How? How do you think that person's prejudice began?

How Do We Become Prejudiced?

Chapter Four
When We're Asleep, We Can't See

Shadows of the Past: A Story

Everyone had gathered in a cave under the ground, its walls lined with cement blocks. They were in darkness except for the flickering light of a big screen. As they sat in rows facing the screen, one movie constantly replayed—*The Shadows of the Past*. In this movie, every event of the past flickered across the screen, showing what the people in the audience had been doing all their lives, as well as what their ancestors, and their ancestors' ancestors had accomplished. Behind the people, above their heads, a long row of movie projectors were aimed at the screens. Each person watching wore gray clothing, and the light from the screen reflected on the dark gray-colored lenses of their glasses.

Yanno, seated in one of the long rows, got an urge to do something that he was sure was forbidden. It was something no one had ever done before. Still, he could not control the urge. He turned around and *looked* at the projectors. In that moment, his gray-colored glasses cracked! Turning back to the big screen, he saw that the crack interfered with the ongoing pictures of the ancestors. He thought there was something wrong and tried to rub his eyes. As he did, he the glasses fell off and hit the floor with a crash.

As he bent forward to look for them, he groped around blindly until he found only the bare frames and broken glass. Yanno put on the frames and looked around. What he saw amazed him. There were rows of people staring up at a gigantic screen, all wearing glasses with gray-colored lenses! He had never noticed this before and was shocked. How could he have participated with all these people in watching images of the past without ever having realized it before? How could he have spent his entire life never wanting, before now, to ask why they were doing this?

Yanno looked behind him at the wall and saw the rows of projectors flickering. Half blindly, he got up and moved about. This startled others around him, who yelled at him to sit down. He was disturbing their show. A few minutes ago, he would have been one of them, yelling at someone else to sit down, but now, without the glasses on, he had suddenly had an insight. Something had changed. His thoughts were different.

As Yanno moved abruptly, he accidentally bumped into Jenna, who tripped and fell, losing her glasses, too. She saw Yanno make his way through the row of people in gray-colored glasses and decided to follow him as he groped toward the flickering light of the projectors. She wasn't sure why she felt the need to follow him, but she knew she could no longer remain where she was.

The floor was on an incline, and Yanno found himself on a ramp that forced him to creep on all fours. He felt compelled to keep moving toward the flickering light. As he moved closer, he ran into a wall. The light was too high for him to reach. He moved to his left and along the wall, hoping it would lead somewhere. After a long while, he came to a dead end.

Exhausted, Yanno put his full weight on the wall to rest for a moment. Jenna, who had now made her way to the wall, noticed a thin shaft of light that seemed to be coming through a crack, from the other side of the wall.

"What's that light?" she asked Yanno. At that moment, Yanno felt a metal bar across the wall, and pushed it. The heavy wall gave way and suddenly became a door. With its blinding brilliance, the light outside overwhelmed the two of them. They covered their eyes with their hands.

Behind them angry voices demanded that the light be stopped! Stumbling through the secret passage they had found, the two escaped prisoners moved beyond this apparent exit and shut the heavy door behind them.

Yanno stood there for a long time, unable to see anything. Little by little his eyes became adjusted to the brightness, and he finally was able to make out certain forms. He put his hands over his eyes and peeked through his fingers, trying to make sense of what he was seeing. Their exit was, in fact, an entryway into a new world.

Jenna was amazed that she was no longer in an underground cave. There was no screen with projected images on the wall, no endless shadows of the past, no feeling of the constant anxiety she had felt before. Before her was a green field that stretched out before them with leafy-green trees and a brilliant blue sky. They knelt down in the soft, damp grass in complete wonder! The smell of exotic flowers permeated their beings. They both became lost in the beautiful aroma.

In the far reaches of Jenna's mind she felt a flicker of familiarity, as if she had been there before, a long, long time ago. What had been real for her moments ago now seemed like a nightmare from which she was finally awaking. In the brilliance of this moment she felt totally new, as if she were a child again.

Yanno began to think about his former life back in the cave, with the shadows of their ancestors, the endless drama of repetition, as well as the fear and constant danger it had brought him. He felt that fear now, but recognized in that moment that it was no longer real. He saw that every fear he had felt in his life was nothing more than a memory. In the brilliance of this wondrous light that surrounded him, he could no longer hold on to that fear. Yanno recognized that, all this time, he had been asleep, hypnotized by dark glasses, big-screen dramas, and the fear of dreams.

Jenna felt a tremendous sadness overcome her, an overwhelming grief for those still locked in the cave. She could see clearly now. Yanno and Jenna understood that they had been living in the shadows of their long departed ancestors. They had been looking at projected images on a screen—a screen they had mistaken for real life.

They knew they were awake now and hoped they could help others see how they had been put to sleep by the gray-colored glasses that had been put on them when they were only children, and how the glasses slowly but steadily had robbed them of the light—of their youth.

Now, Jenna and Yanno were free. They vowed to never wear gray-colored glasses again, and to tell everyone they were about to meet what they had learned.

Hypnosis: The Power of Suggestion

Have you ever seen people hypnotized, in real life or maybe on a television show? It's something like being prejudiced. Here's why. The hypnotist "puts you to sleep" and tells you that when you wake up, at his or her command, you'll do something you're asked to do. Maybe you'll be asked to crow like a rooster or bark like a dog. This is called a "post-hypnotic suggestion," doing something *after* you're supposedly "awakened" but in fact are still under the spell of the hypnotist.

The really amazing thing is that when the person being hypnotized is "awakened" and is given a "post-hypnotic suggestion" and does it, he or she is *not aware* of being hypnotized—even when asked afterward. In the end, a hypnotized subject, about to be really awakened, is told he or she will feel refreshed and have no memory of what happened. And that's usually exactly what happens.

So how does prejudice work like hypnosis? Look at the steps:

1. When you're hypnotized, you "go to sleep," becoming unaware of the reality of the world around you.
2. You do something, often something foolish, simply because someone tells you to do it, not because you really want to.
3. You react to the images your mind presents as if they were real, unaware that you've been hypnotized.

Doesn't that sound like being prejudiced?

Time to Wake Up

Many people remain "asleep," thinking that life as they perceive it is real. But sometimes it isn't, and one of the times is when we're acting out of prejudice. Acting with prejudice is like acting in a bad drama, or a bad dream in our brains that has been played out for centuries, passed from one generation to the next.

This bad dream is nothing more than a movie like *Shadows of the Past*. These shadows are memories of what has gone before, memories of our forgotten tribal ancestors who created this soap opera-like drama.

For example, in many cases men were brought up to feel superior and to treat women as if they were inferior. Our male ancestors generally believed that women were the "weaker sex, " inferior, and they believed their perceptions were real. These ancestors passed this attitude on to me. I was taught to believe that women are incapable of doing what men can do, generally less intelligent, and not able to hold a job of great importance. I was taught that a woman's place is in the home—cooking, raising children, and keeping house. Men went to work; they were strong, in control, and far more capable of great accomplishments of any kind. I was conditioned to believe this, and did for many years. The very idea of "women's liberation" frightened me; when I first heard that expression I was wearing gray-colored glasses.

Sometimes when you feel fear, however, you are awakened to a new realization.

Up to that point I had thought that my conditioned views of women were the truth. But I was wrong.

When I look back now, I can see that women were angry inside. Just as men were programmed to act superior, women acted polite because they were *programmed* to be nice, to avoid showing their real feelings. I felt that they secretly resented male authority over them and showed it in ways that were hidden.

I was so brainwashed to "act like a man" that I didn't realize that I was acting unfairly toward women. I felt trapped by how I was supposed to act—to automatically hold doors open for women, to assume that they were the "weaker sex" and that I had to do everything for them, to feel I had to always be in charge—in control.

I now understand that I was prejudiced by my elders when I was young. I suspect that I felt something was wrong with being prejudiced, but no one ever helped me realize what was happening, because they, too, were locked into their prejudices that made them feel safe, that life was predictable, and orderly. But as I grew up, I made an important discovery.

DISCOVERY 12
Acting in prejudiced ways is not orderly or safe.
It is acting out of ignorance.

The Effect of Brainwashing

Supposedly used with success by the Communists in the early 1950s during the Korean War, the process of "brainwashing" is said to cleanse the mind of its original beliefs so that new beliefs might be substituted. This process may sound painless, but the techniques used on captured servicemen in that and later wars were often brutal.

Think of what it must be like to be a prisoner of war, isolated from companions and deprived of food and sleep. Imagine being endlessly badgered with constant political propaganda over periods of weeks and months, even years. After such treatment, some captives were induced to publicly "confess" that they had been fighting for an unjust cause. They were brainwashed into turning their backs on their country and cause.

It's difficult to imagine what choices we would make in that situation. Hopefully, we will never have to find out. But to understand prejudice, we must question our own conditioning—examine those beliefs that seem acceptable on the surface, but that at their roots are simply unfounded prejudices. Do we have just grounds for everything we believe? Do we have sufficient knowledge to act upon our point of view?

Like indoctrination through brainwashing, we are often conditioned—in more subtle ways over longer periods of time—to accept what we are taught without questioning. But we can become aware that we've been asleep—and then wake up!

DISCOVERY 13
When we become prejudiced by not being aware, we become numb to life around us. We accept the opinions of other people without finding out the facts for ourselves.

Becoming Aware of Our Prejudiced Thinking

There are many examples of prejudices inherited from our tribal ancestors, and they are so ingrained in our thinking that we don't even notice that they're there!

As you look at the following examples of prejudice, maintain your scientific method of understanding; explore all avenues of thought and try your best to respond honestly.

ASK YOURSELF
Do I have any of these prejudiced thoughts?

If you do, make this an opportunity to learn about yourself rather than to protect yourself from an unpleasant realization. Look honestly at the prejudiced thoughts you may have, and understand that you can change your thinking, if you want to. Think about these common prejudices:

Men are naturally more intelligent than women.
Women are kinder and gentler than men.
White people are better business people than black people.
Black people are more athletic than white people.
Younger people are better workers than older people.
To have peace, we must fight for it.
Authorities should never be questioned.
To be good we must do what we're told to do.
Ambition is good; winning is everything.
The more money you have, the better person you must be.

Can you think of others? Which come closest to feelings or opinions that you have? Can you figure out why you have them? Do you believe they are really true? Can you test them to determine whether they're factual?

The Phenomenon of Phobias

Anxious feelings can cause a person to experience fear, tension, and danger. In some cases, the anxiety grows strong enough to be called a "phobia," an exaggerated, usually unexplainable and illogical fear of a person, place or thing, or group of things. Some examples of phobias are:

agoraphobia, a fear of open spaces and crowded places
acrophobia, a fear of heights
claustrophobia, a fear of enclosed places

These phobias produce distorted images in the mind; what we fear is not real, but simply a product of this distortion. In a similar manner, prejudice based on

a dislike of foreigners, can cause us to see anyone different or outside our group as a threat to our safety and security. Have you experienced this "phobia"? What happens is the brain turns this "someone different" into "someone threatening." That person, perhaps without your ever speaking to him or her, seems to us an enemy.

The Only Enemy

Let's say that someone taught you to believe that people who live on the other side of your street are no good. If you believe what you've been conditioned to think is real, then what is "real" to you (to your brain) is that all those people are "enemies," that they are a threat to the way you think and live.

Feeling threatened, you may believe it's necessary to defend yourself. And it's easy to see that once you've decided you must defend yourself and your family or group against them, *you* are creating conflict. Carrying this conflict inside you, chances are you'll sooner or later get into a skirmish with someone across the street. If you constantly feel you must defend yourself against this "enemy," it's very likely you will!

Can you see how this happens? Look at this process:

The Ten Mental Steps to Conflict

1. That person across the street is no good.
2. That person is different from me.
3. That person is "my enemy."
4. That person is a threat to my safety and security.
5. That person is a threat to my family or group.
6. I must defend myself against my enemy.
7. I must defend my group against "them"!
8. I feel inner conflict.
9. I project my conflict onto my "enemy."
10. Sooner or later we're going to fight!

DISCOVERY 14
There's only one enemy, the one we create in our brain!

Band-Aids and Revolving Doors

Many people are aware of the damage prejudice can cause, but look for solutions as if the problem were a small one or an individual one. They think of it as "his problem," or "my family's" problem and don't know how to deal with it effectively. One method they use is a "band-aid" solution—applying a tiny band-aid to cover the huge wound that prejudice creates. For example, suppose you have a friend who tells nasty jokes about people of another color or religion. You suspect he's prejudiced, and it bothers you, but you tell yourself: "I just won't laugh at his jokes and he'll see that I don't think they're funny and quit telling them." This is a "band-aid" solution; your friend probably has deep prejudices, and after reading this book, you can help him escape from them.

ASK YOURSELF
**When have I used a "band-aid" to try to cover
a huge wound created by prejudice?**

Others use a "revolving-door" approach. They keep going around and around the same problem, never fixing it because they never really face it. Suppose your brother dislikes the family across the street. This is a problem for you because a young girl in the family is in your class at school and seems pretty nice. You think: "I really would like to make friends with her, but my brother says her family's no good. If we become friends, it will simply mean trouble. So I better not." Every time you have a chance to make friends with her, you think the same thing, and never really face the real question: "What's she really like?"

ASK YOURSELF
**When have I gone around and around the same problem,
like a revolving door, without figuring out a solution?**

How do we become prejudiced? We look without really trying to understand, act based on images our brains been conditioned to see, and create enemies that actually exist only in our brains. How many of us do this?
All of us!

IN-SIGHTS

★ Yanno and Jenna are two characters in the story who were "asleep" during their lives and didn't recognize how they had been conditioned—until their gray-colored glasses broke.

★ Being prejudiced is a lot like being "put to sleep" by a hypnotist. We act on suggestions made by the hypnotist according to images that exist only in our brains.

★ Our ancestors brought up their children to believe that men are superior to women. This is just one example of prejudiced thinking that we probably have inherited.

★ We are "asleep" when we accept the opinions of others without finding out the facts for ourselves.

★ We see another person as an "enemy" when our brain has been conditioned to see that person in that way.

★ When we see someone as different from us, we may feel that our safety is threatened. Feeling threatened, we defend ourselves, which puts us immediately into conflict.

★ A "band-aid" solution tries to cover up a huge wound—such as the damage caused by prejudice—with the equivalent of a tiny band-aid.

★ The "revolving-door" approach to a problem means going around and around it without really facing it to find a solution.

★ How do we become prejudiced? We look without really trying to understand, act based on images our brains been conditioned to see, and create enemies that actually exist only in our brains.

THINKING FOR YOURSELF

✦ What do you think is the meaning of the story *Shadows of the Past?*

✦ Do you think Yanno and Jenna had been brainwashed to believe things that weren't true?

✦ Do you think you've been conditioned to believe something that you suspect may not be true?

✦ Do you think your conditioning has affected the way you think about things? In what way?

✦ Do you think many people are walking through life without really seeing?

✦ Why do you think these people are going through their lives this way?

✦ Are there people around you who are obviously prejudiced and seem completely unaware of it?

✦ Can you recall a time you felt "superior" or "inferior" to someone? How did it make you feel? How do you think the other person felt?

✦ Do you think it's true that we accept the opinions of other people without finding out the facts for ourselves? When is the last time you did that?

✦ Have you used "band-aid therapy" or the "revolving-door approach" in your life? Have you seen them used by anyone else? What was the situation?

Chapter Five
The Bells and Knots of Conditioning

The "Fight or Flight" Response

Can you imagine how hard it would be to have to decide whether to run away to save your life, or to stay and defend your home? Wouldn't this create enormous conflict inside you? Such difficult decisions are made every day in countries where some groups are subject to violent acts by others, and whose governments are powerless to defend them. In fact, in some countries the government is made up of the prejudiced members of one group and supports brutal acts against another group.

Here where we live, and where life is not so dramatic, we are prejudiced as well. Even though our prejudices may not result in violent acts against other groups, they have the same root causes and can result in needless hurt and damage. Our prejudice often springs from something that scares us and causes us to want to protect ourselves.

For example, suppose you're walking down the street and you see a huge, mean-looking brown dog. Its ears are back and it's showing its large, sharp teeth. It's growling, and looks as if it's going to attack you. What's your first response? What happens inside you? A signal of fear registers in your brain because of the danger the dog seems to represent. Your brain sends messages to your body to prepare for one of two actions: fight, or run away.

This is called the "fight or flight" response. It's how your body has learned to deal with this situation, for the same reason we've been talking about all along—your brain wants you to survive.

> **DISCOVERY 15**
> The "fight or flight" response is there for self-preservation.
> It's an instinct to protect you from harm,
> which is a healthy and natural response to *real* danger.

Now suppose a few weeks later, you see another big brown dog . It looks almost exactly like the first mean dog, but this one is wagging its tail. What would immediately happen in your brain? Even though this dog is wagging its tail, you feel afraid. This is a conditioned reaction. Your brain is recreating a threatening image of the first dog that growled at you.

If we take apart the word "prejudice" we see that *pre* means "before," and *judice* relates to "judgment," or "opinion." So, prejudice is a pre-judgment, an opinion already formed. Your reaction to the big brown dog is based on a prejudgment, a opinion your brain holds based on its experience with the first brown dog. Since your original action, based on your encounter with the mean-looking brown dog, was to either fight (defend yourself) or flee (run away), your reaction now, based on memory of that incident, is identical, even though the dog is friendly. That same would be true of my brain, anyone's brain. This is simply how the human brain operates: Your first encounter with a growling big brown dog prejudiced you to believe that you need to defend yourself against *all* big brown dogs. You are prejudiced!

Although we all may have grown up in different places and we've had different experiences, the brain works the same for all of us. To protect itself in a conflict situation, it cues us either to get ready for a battle or to run away. The next time you start thinking about how different someone is from you, stop and remember what we all have in common: When we're scared, we either want to fight, or run away.

Fear Makes Negative Images Stick

Depending on your past experience with dogs, you'll respond to the new, friendly dog in one of two ways:

1. You see the dog as he is: "His tail is wagging. He's friendly. No need to defend myself or run away"; or
2. Even though the dog is acting friendly, you react based on a prejudment—prejudice: "He's going to attack me!"

In this case, the memory of the mean dog was so scary, it stuck in your brain. Maybe you were bitten by a dog before and are frightened of dogs in general. Whatever the case, if your brain produces an image of the old mean dog when you look at the new dog, you'll be reacting in a prejudiced way. Instead of acting based on what we really see, we react based on remembered fears.

Pavlov's Dogs

Have you ever heard of "Pavlov's dogs"? Ivan Pavlov was a Russian surgeon who developed the concept of the "conditioned reflex." In a well-known experiment, every time he fed his dog, he would ring a bell. Right before the dog was fed, no matter what time of day, Pavlov would ring a bell.

Over time, the dog came to understand that when he heard a bell, he was going to eat. The dog came to associate the bell with the approach of mealtime. So, when the dog heard the bell, he would salivate. He produced water at the mouth in expectation of the delicious food. Then, Pavlov would feed him.

One day, to try something different, Pavlov rang the bell but didn't give the dog food. What amazed the scientist is that the dog salivated anyway. Days later, when Pavlov again rang the bell, even though the dog didn't know if he was going to get food or not, he would salivate!

So, Pavlov discovered that he had conditioned his dog to salivate—to react in a certain way—by creating an association between the sound of a bell and food.

In our daily life, people often "ring" a certain "bell" that we react to without thinking. For example, if someone calls you a name you don't like, is there a kind of bell that goes off inside you, making you want to fight or run away? If someone tells you to do something you don't want to do, does a bell inside ring with anger? Fear? Shame? These are the ways we become prejudiced:

We're trained to prejudge instead of see things as they are.
We're programmed to react instead of act.
We're conditioned to fight or to run away.

Taught by His Students

Have you ever heard of B.F. Skinner? He was a psychologist who became famous for studying human conditioning and the way people respond to rewards and punishments. But he was also a teacher.

One day, his students wound up teaching *him* something about conditioning. The students got together before class and developed a plan. They were all aware that Professor Skinner, when he taught, was a pacer. While he lectured, he paced up and down the front of the classroom. So, they devised a plan based on their scientific hypothesis—that they had the power to get him to stand on only one side of the classroom!

That day, whenever Professor Skinner walked to the right side of the room as he was teaching, the students would listen attentively and raise their hands to ask many questions. But when he walked to the left side of the room as he paced, the students would act bored, not ask questions and didn't pay attention.

By the end of the class, Professor Skinner, who normally paced back and forth continually, was pinned up against—you guessed it—the right side of the room! Professor Skinner liked hearing the positive remarks and responded well to the rewards his students gave him. The lesson for the day was that conditioning works through the use of rewards and punishments.

The Atomic Bomb Drills

As we've already seen, we're conditioned by so many things in our everyday life that sometimes we're not even aware of them.

In the late 1940s and 1950s, a drill called an "air raid alert" was held regularly at American schools. The drill was supposed to practice protective actions to be taken in case of an atomic bomb attack by the Soviet Union, "the Russians." When a school's siren sounded, the students, like Pavlov's dog, were taught to react in a conditioned way: they ducked under their desks.

These drills took place in schools all over the United States during what was called the "Cold War"—cold, because there was no actual war. Still, it was a time when Russia and the United States each felt threatened by the other. The Russian felts that the U.S., with its powerful nuclear weapons, would be tempted to attack them; we felt that their "Godless Communist" system of government was out to destroy us. Such great prejudices could easily have led to the use of atomic weapons—World War III or even the end of the world.

Fortunately, we never went to war with the Soviet Union. But because of what people in the U. S. were taught to believe about Russians, combined with the fear of atomic bomb attacks and sirens going off as a signal for everyone to hide, some students became conditioned to react to Russians in a fearful, hateful way. It was the same for Russian children—they were conditioned to hate and fear people of the United States.

In the 1970s, the residents of a California town called Sebastopol contacted a town in Russia of the same name. It turns out that the California town had actually been named by Russian settlers in the 1800s and the town's present residents wanted a "Sister City" relationship with the Russian people, both to recognize their heritage and to help foster peace between the two countries.

Some of the Russians responded by visiting the U.S. town. Many people in the California town were nervous, because to them the Russians were still "the enemy"—an image of Russians that automatically popped into their heads because of Cold War attitudes and all those air raid drills.

When the Russians arrived, however, they were not what the Californians had expected. They were dressed like Americans, looked like Americans, walked like Americans—and some spoke better English!

The Californians were confused. They weren't sure what they'd expected to see — perhaps huge men dressed in military uniforms and carrying guns. Their brains were engaged in an inner struggle, trying to reconcile the image of Russians held there with the people they were actually seeing.

One of those Americans was me. At a gathering to get acquainted with our visitors, I recall being too afraid to speak with one of "them." Instead, I turned my attention to a small, pretty, shy lady, who returned my hello. When I said that it was interesting to have Russians visit us, I was shocked when she relied, "Oh, yes, and *we* are glad to be here." I had thought that she was one of our Sebastolpol group, but in a split second she became "one of them"—my supposed enemy!

In that next moment, I had a "fight or flight" reaction. I froze and felt myself feel the urge to protect myself or run away. The bell in my brain was ringing loud and clear. "Watch out! This is your enemy!"

While all this was going on in my head, on the outside I'm pretty sure I wasn't showing anything except embarrassment for not knowing that she wasn't from our town. But inside my stomach knotted up, my palms were sweating, my eyes widened, and my heart was beating fast! I was ready to fight her, or to run away from this threat.

False Image, False Alarm

But where was the threat? Certainly it was not coming from the young lady who was standing before me. She wasn't big or wearing a military uniform or carrying a gun. She didn't look frightening at all. So what was making me feel and act as if she were a threat to me? What was making me prepare to fight or to run away?

It was my prejudiced vision of Russians, conditioned by years of repeated judgments. But now, right in front of me, was reality, in the form of a real person who was nothing like the enemy my conditioned mind had envisioned. And she spoke perfect English!

I shall never forget that evening. We had a warm and interesting conversation and I enjoyed myself thoroughly. I have since traveled to Russia and found Russians to be wonderful people who want peace as much as we do. I now have loving friends there.

Has my conditioning disappeared? While the computer in my mind still has some memory of conditioned images, I no longer have the reactions I had that night when I made new Russian acquaintances. That experience alone taught me much about the power of prejudice. It showed me how someone can fear and hate other people—even to the point of believing it is necessary to kill them—all because of images the conditioned mind presents, images with no basis in reality.

That night I was filled with joy over my discovery and, at the same time, filled with sadness when I became clearly aware of many people who fear and hate, and want to protect themselves against "enemies" that live and breathe only inside their own heads.

ASK YOURSELF
Have I created an enemy inside my head?
Did I realize at the time that I was acting out of prejudice?

DISCOVERY 16
Unaware of our programming, we act as if our hatred is necessary.
But we are the ones who are keeping it alive.

If we want to, we can not hate. All it takes is a conscious decision to become aware of when we are acting based on a real situation, and when we are reacting only to an imagined fear.

The Prejudice Knot

Have you ever seen a mobius strip? Can you see how endless its route is? It's hard to tell where it begins and where it ends—or if it ever does.

If you've ever pulled your shoelace into a knot, you know how difficult it can be to untie it. The same thing happens when our thoughts that get knotted up in our brain. Unless we become aware of what has happened, we could stay there—with our thoughts knotted up—forever.

Knotted-up thoughts in the brain like prejudice can cause confusion and hurt the person thinking them, as well as anyone who is the object of that thinking. And because neither person is aware of it, the knot could stay tied for a long, long time. What holds the knot of prejudice together? Conditioned thinking!

How does it start? Usually, with a basic statement of "information." Somehow, a thought is expressed that is not true, or is only partially true, or is meant to hide the truth. Once that thought is "out there," people hear it, repeat, and begin to believe in it more and more—and prejudice is born.

A Failure to

Communicate

How the Prejudice Knot Get Tied Up

1. *A basic thought becomes a statement of "information."*

"You know, I think that all people with blue skins are mean, greedy, and distrustful.

2. *The statement is accepted without question and repeated by others.*

"All people with blue skins are mean, greedy, and distrustful. I know this because I heard it from my best friend."

3. *As the thought is expressed by more people, it becomes an accepted belief.*

"Everybody says that people with blue skin are mean, greedy, and distrustful. Since so many people say so, it must be true. I don't have much experience with blue people myself, but who am I to disagree with so many others with experience? They're the ones who know."

4. *The belief provokes a reaction.*

"Since people with blue skin are mean, greedy, and distrustful. I shouldn't put up with such people—not even tolerate them. I'll avoid having anything to do with blue-skinned people, but if they do something bad to me, I'll get back at them!"

5. *The knot gets tighter and tighter.*

"I hate blue-skinned people, so they must hate me back. I should protect myself in case they try to do something to me. I'll join other people who think the way I do, so we can feel safe and secure. Together we can defend ourselves, our families, and our country against all those mean, greedy, and distrustful blue-skinned people.

"Why must we defend ourselves against blue-skinned people? Because they threaten our values and beliefs, our customs and traditions, our heritage, and our nation—everything we stand for!"

How did we become so prejudiced—our thinking so tightly tied into a knot? Remembered fear creates negative images that get stuck in our minds. Like reacting to the bells that Pavlov rang to condition his dog, we create our "enemy" and we create our "hate." And we blame others when *we're* the ones who are responsible.

IN-SIGHTS

★ The "fight or flight" response is one in which our brain prepares our body to either fight or to run away, to ensure our survival.

★ Ivan Pavlov was a Russian surgeon who developed the concept of the "conditioned reflex."

★ Pavlov discovered that he could condition a dog to respond in a certain way—just by ringing a bell.

★ We humans are "programmed" beings as well; each of us has certain "bells" that set off conditioned reactions inside us.

★ We're conditioned by so many things in our everyday life that sometimes we're not even aware of them.

★ Most of us are conditioned to fear and hate, and to want to protect ourselves against a projected "enemy" that has been programmed inside our heads.

★ Unaware of this programming, we act as if our hatred is necessary. But we are the ones who carry it on, from the conditioning of our Forgotten Ancestors.

★ Unless we become aware of how our thoughts have been tied into a unending knot, we could stay tied in that knot forever.

★ The never-ending knot of prejudice is held together by one thing: conditioned thinking.

★ Prejudice begins with a basic statement of "information" that is not true, or not completely true. Repeated frequently over time it becomes an accepted, unquestioned belief.

★ Over time, many people have become tied so tightly in the knot of prejudice that they think it is impossible to get free of it.

THINKING FOR YOURSELF

✦ When was the last time you felt the "fight or flight" response? What was the situation? What was the outcome?

✦ What do you think of Pavlov and his experiment? Do you think the discovery of the conditioned reflex was important? Why?

✦ Were you amazed to find out that the ringing of a bell could cause a dog to salivate, even when the dog didn't get food?

✦ What are some "bells" that cause you to act in a conditioned way? Have you been angry, scared, or excited recently? About what? What were the bells that set you off?

✦ What people have you seen who are conditioned to hate or to fear other people? Any people in the news? Any people in your own community? In another part of the world?

✦ Have you heard any comments lately that you would consider prejudiced? What were they? How did you feel when you heard them?

✦ Can you see how a basic statement of "information" can sound truer as more people accept it? Do you think that could be dangerous? Why?

✦ When you hear such a statement of "information," does it occur to you to question it, or do you generally accept what you hear as true?

✦ Does your acceptance of information depend on who's giving it to you? Whose information would you not question? Whose information would you immediately question? Why?

✦ Do you believe the knot of prejudice can tie us up forever? What steps can we take to untie it?

Chapter Six
Elements of Knotted Thinking

Defective Wiring in Our Brain

Over time our brain, like a worn-out mechanical device, can cause trouble because its wiring is defective. Our knotted thinking keeps us from seeing things as they really are. Wouldn't it be wonderful if we could cut through our knots and become able to think clearly all the time? Sometimes people who cut through the knots—who "wake up"— discover that for most of their lives they've believed something that's not true.

To help us move in that direction, let's take a good look at the ways our thinking becomes knotted, for these are the ways we become prejudiced. Learning to recognize them and how they work can help free us from the knots.

Repetition is hearing the same thing over and over, and saying it to others whether true or not.

When something is repeated often, we feel compelled to believe it is true simply because we've heard it so many times. This is how advertisers try to make us buy their products. Ads for a huge variety of products are shown on TV or aired on the radio time and time again, or plastered on signs and billboards everywhere. Billions of dollars are being spent to condition us to buy. If repetition didn't work to make us believe something, do you think advertisers would continue to spend so much money?

Comparison is the process of comparing one group of people with another.

This leads to viewing ourselves as "us" and everyone else as "them." Thinking in this manner leads us to judge or "rank" the various groups we know as "better" or "worse," as "superior" or "inferior," and there is a natural tendency to place ourselves at the top of the list. Such thinking causes people to adhere to their own group, to separate from one another.

Projection is the act of "throwing" the image in our minds onto another person.

This works in the same way that a projector "throws" an image of a movie onto a screen. We assume, for example, that if we dislike blue-skinned people because they are mean, greedy, and distrustful, they must dislike us in return.

Who am I?

If they hate us, they are our enemy. So when we encounter a blue-skinned person, we project their dislike of us onto them; we think to ourselves: "Blue skin? My enemy!"

Identification is conforming to the ways and values of a group for security and support.

Many of us join organizations to gain a sense of security. We identify with certain organizations, belief systems, political parties, ethnic groups, or nations because we feel comfortable knowing that we are with others who think as we do. We believe that "belonging" protects us against others who oppose our beliefs. We belong in order to survive. Remember the story of how the Rock Tribe began and how it progressed from a small group to a large culture, staying together for safety? What held the tribe together was identification—individuals thinking like other members of the group, becoming conditioned to think, act, and even look like other group members.

We still do this today. A person's "identity" is often made up of their experiences with the various groups they belong to. Unconsciously imitating a group's "personality" helps members feel "accepted" by the group, which provides them feelings of security and belonging. Think of the groups you belong to and how belonging makes you feel.

When we identify with a particular group, we take on the personality of the group. It's something like putting on a costume, going to a costume party, and pretending to be someone different—or acting out a role we've memorized in play. But in a play or at a costume party, we're *conscious of* what we're doing. We're aware that the costume or the role is not really who we are. We want to create an illusion of reality, so that our character is believable, but we know that the play is not real. Yet when we're "unconsciously conditioned" to put on the particular "face" or "costume" of a social group, it's as if we're acting without realizing it, looking at life through darkened glasses. But this is not a play; it is our lives!

Authority refers to believing and obeying those we think to have the power to tell us what to believe and what to do.

When we accept information that "experts" say is true and right, without finding out for ourselves—without asking questions— we are surrendering to authority. However, some authorities have our best interests at heart, while others do not.

A person who owns a greenhouse and sells us the right garden plants for the type of soil and sunshine we have may be called an authority on plants. A doctor who specializes in heart transplants is obviously an authority in that field. These are examples of authorities we sometimes have to rely on in this busy world, where there never seems to be enough time to learn everything we need to know.

The kind of authority we need to watch out for is someone who claims to know what's best for us and wants to condition us into believing what he or she says is the truth. Ever watch "infomercials" on TV? Don't those "experts" have a wealth of information? Don't they seem smart and sincere? Don't they seem to have our best interests at heart? Yet we know, when the telephone numbers come up in the screen and they tell us to get out our credit cards that what they really want is our money.

Other "experts" seek publicity rather than money, while still others are hungry for political power. How can we tell which ones to believe if we don't ask questions? For example, we've all listened to politicians trying to persuade us to believe their promises and points of view. Here are some questions we might want to ask ourselves about them:

1. Is it possible that their primary goal might be simply to get into office?
2. Do they seem sincere in their beliefs, or would they probably change their minds if they thought most voters disagreed with them?
3. Might they be *too* sincere in their beliefs, so that they would support punishing or killing those who disagreed with them?
4. If you want peace and feel deeply that war is not acceptable, will this person support your belief that there are more intelligent ways to resolve conflict?
5. How much do you think they believe what they say they believe. How do you know? How will you find out?

From an early age, we are conditioned to accept authority. An "Inner Authority"—a voice inside us—tells us what to think, what to say, and how to live, according to a certain set of values that may be based on race or culture or national origin. An "Outer Authority"—the leaders and role models of our group—plays on our "Inner Authority," appealing to the ideas and feelings we've been programmed to believe will bring us security and happiness.

Reinforcement *is using rewards or punishments to modify behavior*

You might reward your pet by offering it some praise or food; you might punish what you consider bad behavior with scolding words and punitive actions. This giving of rewards and punishment is meant to achieve a certain effect—to get your pet to behave, in a way that pleases you, not necessarily a way that is natural for the animal.

Have you ever been punished for doing something an authority figure didn't want you to do? Have you ever been rewarded for acting heroically or being smart? When an Outer Authority wants you to think and act in certain ways, he or she may already know how you've been conditioned to act and may be fully aware of what "buttons" to push to cause the Inner Authority to make you think and act in those ways.

Belief *is something we accept to be true without examining it for ourselves.*

It doesn't make sense to believe what someone else tells us without finding out for ourselves whether it is really true. Still, we often do, simply because checking into the truth of everything we hear is a lot of work. So we become selective; we check into the facts when we are really curious about something, or when it is in our own interest. Other times, however, we simply "go with the flow," believing what our friends or authorities tell us. After all, our lazy brains tells us, if so many people say so, it must be true.

DISCOVERY 17
**There are many authorities who can be of help to you
throughout your life. But it's important to be able to tell the difference
between authorities who have your best interests at heart
and those who do not.**

ELEMENTS OF KNOTTED THINKING

NAME	ACTION	EXAMPLE
Repetition	Saying or hearing the same thing over and over. so that it sounds true.	"The best part of waking up is Folgers in your cup."
Comparison	Comparing one group of people with another.	"People with blue skin are not as smart as we are."
Projection	"Throwing" an image in our minds onto another person or thing.	"I don't like blue-skinned people, so they must hate me. They're the enemy."
Identification	Conforming to the ways and values of a group for security and support.	"My group doesn't hang out with blue-skinned people. We stick together."
Authority	Accepting authority without question.	"All you have to do is just what I tell you. I know what's best."
Reinforcement	Rewarding or punishing to achieve a certain behavior.	"You're a good kid. Just do what I say and you'll get money. Otherwise, you'll get nothing!"
Belief	Accepting something with no proof that it's true.	"Our ways are the only right ways. Everyone I know says so."

Prejudice develops in our minds through any and all of these devices. It may start with an untrue idea that when repeated seems true. These wrong ideas cause us to judge others around us, including new people we meet, and to project onto them our mind's image of what they are like. Our ideas usually conform to those of our group or result from obedience to authorities whose opinions and rules we fail to question. And our prejudices are constantly reinforced by punishments and rewards, used by our group leaders and other authorities to keep us thinking and acting the way they believe we should.

Our Ancestors Are Us

You and I were born into a world already full of conditioned and prejudiced thinking. The culture we were born into programs us and continues to do so on a daily basis. Thus many things we believe today may be part of a "tribal inheritance" we've claimed as our birthright without question. Perhaps we should ask ourselves:

1. If who we are is only a hand-me-down set of tribal customs, how do we find out whether they're valid, and if they still work for us today?
2. We all have some kind of belief system. How do we find out for ourselves what having a belief system really means?
3. If we're acting in a prejudiced way and aren't aware of it, don't we want to become aware of it, so we can actively make some changes?

DISCOVERY 18
A problem created by prejudice is not "your" problem,
"my" problem, or even "our" problem.
It is *the* problem, for it affects us all.

IN-SIGHTS

★ At some point in their lives, many people make the discovery that up until then they've believed something that is not true.

★ Learning how our thinking becomes knotted can helps us understand and guard against conditioning.

★ **Repetition** is saying the same thing over and over. This is how television advertisers get us to buy their products.

★ **Comparison** is the process of comparing one person with another, or one group of people with another. Thinking in this manner, we judge or "rank" our group as "superior" and others as "inferior."

★ **Projection** is "throwing" the image in our minds onto another person in the same way that a projector "throws" an image of a movie onto a screen. But is the image true or real?

★ **Identification** is conforming to the ways and values of a group. We do this because it makes us feel safe and secure, like being members of a family. The leaders of our groups become our role models and authorities.

★ **Authority** refers to accepting without questioning what we are told by those we think have the power to tell us. When we accept information from "experts" without asking questions, we are sleepily surrendering to their conditioning— becoming obedient. When deciding whether to be obedient, we must be able to tell the difference between authorities who are truly helping us and those who are not.

★ **Reinforcement** is using rewards or punishments to modify behavior. From being yelled at for disobeying our parents to being rewarded for good behavior, we are subject to conditioning through reinforcement throughout our lives.

★ **Belief** is something we accept to be true without examining it for ourselves.

★ Conditioning is not education. It is a way of developing habits. Only when we are receiving intelligent guidance to help us make informed decisions can we consider ourselves being educated.

★ Any problem created by prejudice is not "your" problem, "my problem," or even "our problem." It's *the* problem, for it affects us all.

THINKING FOR YOURSELF

✦ Have you ever discovered that something you've always believed isn't true? What was it? How did you find out and how did you feel?

✦ Which element(s) of knotted thinking come closest to the kind you've experienced?

✦ Is there someone you may have felt prejudiced toward recently, or someone you felt acted in a prejudiced way toward you? What happened?

✦ What's an element of your knotted thinking that makes you feel confused?

✦ Where have you seen repetition used to condition thinking?

✦ Name some incidents in which you have seen or heard evidence of comparison, projection, or identification. Were you aware of what was happening when you first heard or saw them? Are you aware of them now?

✦ Has obedience to authority ever been a problem for you? Have you ever had trouble dealing with it? Do you think that the problem was with you or the authority?

✦ What are some rewards you've received in your life for obeying or doing "the right thing"? How have you been punished for disobeying someone's instructions, or doing what someone believed was "wrong"? Do you think the reward or punishment was appropriate?

✦ Have you seen evidence that we've been born into a world already conditioned and prejudiced?

Stereotypes

What are the Effects of Our Prejudice?

Chapter Seven

The Conditioned Mind is a Dangerous Mind

We are what we think.
All that we are arise from our thoughts.
With our thoughts we make the world.

How Far Have We Come?

When we look back over the violent history of our race and then hear or read in the news of some horrible thing that someone has done to another, we often ask ourselves, "How far have we come?" and the answer just as often is, "Not far at all." Every day, in at least several parts of the world, there seems to be two opposing sides that cannot come to an agreement and as a result lives are lost. Our scientific minds ask:

Can there ever be agreement when there are always "sides"?

Can there be agreement when tribe-like groups still believe and act according to traditions and customs handed down to them?

If no one identified with either side, wouldn't conflict and violence end? Can it be as simple as that?

Or are people simply far too conditioned, too programmed to see this simple solution?

Here's a summary of the progress you and I have made so far:

1. We've begun to notice the difference between opinion and fact, between assuming and getting information firsthand, and between pre-judging and finding facts.

2. We've looked at our mechanical brains and seen how they've been programmed to create images, many that aren't real or true.

3. We've seen how these images can be formed when we're asleep, under the hypnotic spell of conditioned thinking.

4. We've become aware of how repetition, obedience to authority, and reinforcement work to create false images in our brains, and how we view the world incorrectly through our identification with various groups, stereotyping others, and projecting our wrong images onto them.

5. We've seen how fear creates negative images that get stuck in our brains, and how conditioning takes hold on to these images, forever unless we find a way to wake up.

6. We've discovered, to our amazement, that the hate we feel, passed on to us by our ancestors, is our own invention.

7. We've learned that prejudice is an automatic reaction, and that if we want to act rather than react, we have to think for ourselves.

We have become aware of a lot on our journey of discovery, haven't we? We've learned a great deal about what prejudice is, and how we become prejudiced.

Now we're going to look at the *effects* of prejudice—what happens inside us, outside us, and all around us—when prejudice exists. It's not a pretty picture, but we're determined to learn rather than protect ourselves from the truth, right?

The Words We Use

Most of us can think of at least ten major words that disrespect and dehumanize other people. Many of them are used to put down other racial or ethnic groups. Because these words produce such strong reactions in us, we're not going to use them here. Instead, we'll leave some blank spaces. These spaces signify words that symbolize hatred and prejudice. As you think of the words you know, take a moment—what we might call a Stop! Think! moment—to consider the fear and hatred these words can carry.

_____

_____

_____

_____

_____

_____

A feeling such as hate, or a thought such as "You are my enemy," is triggered by conditioned thinking. When we "feel" that what we think is "right," the thought is enhanced by the feeling. It's so easy to get caught up in this self-protecting treadmill of prejudice.

Thought + Reinforced by Feelings + Words = Action

It is said that "Actions speak louder than words." If someone walks up and punches you, you need no words to realize that this person is angry with you. But what thought, reinforced by feelings and words, led to that action? In everyday conversations, hurtful words are often used. The people who use them are either unaware of the pain they are causing, or fully aware and using them on purpose. Either way, they cause conflict.

Some people think it's fun to use words like these, but if you're ever tempted to use them, it's good to stand in someone else's shoes and ask yourself how you'd feel being called these names.

Here's a game that can help you get firsthand experience of how names can just "pop" into our heads without our even being aware of them. It's called "The Association Game." As you play, let your prejudices just pop out. That way, you'll learn what they are, and you'll be on the path of discovery about what you can do to understand them.

The Association Game

This game tests our ability to observe prejudice in the making. There are many associations that we make every day without thinking. Some of these illustrate our conditioned prejudices by demonstrating our automatic, unconscious reactions to certain words or ideas.

With a friend or family member, take turns calling out the following list of words. The other person must quickly respond with the first word that comes to his or her mind.

For example, if your friend calls out the word "red," what's the first word that comes to your mind? Is it "rose"? Is it "Native American"? "Russian"? Some other word? What do these words tell you about your conditioned brain?

It's a simple game, and it shows the kinds of associations we all make and how deeply ingrained in our thinking these associations exist. You can also play it alone, on paper, using the list below. Ready to give it a try? Write the first word that enters your mind when you see each word. No stopping to think!

Salt _____	War _____	Black _____
Peace _____	Up _____	Enemy _____
In _____	Friend _____	Foreigner _____
Red _____	Black person _____	TV _____
Mexican _____	Hurt _____	Round _____
Fear _____	Asian _____	Obey _____
White person _____	Square _____	Love _____

What others can you think of? The object of the game is to uncover our conditioned thoughts (and feelings that go along with the thoughts), so we can become more aware of thoughts that muddy our brains.

Words Become Attitudes

Using hurtful words is one way we let our prejudices show. Another is thinking in a lazy, sleepy way, and making generalizations about people without taking the time to find out about who they really are.

*A **stereotype** is a standardized mental picture held by members of a group that represents and oversimplified opinion, attitude or judgment.*

Very often it is an oversimplified view of what members of another group are like. This is the result of lazy thinking—it's easier to have a single opinion of a group than opinions about each of its many members—but we will see below how lazy thinking so easily becomes prejudicial thinking.

Below is a list of stereotypes that you can fill in. When you finish, you will probably notice that many of the stereotypes you have in your brain are not flattering. In fact, don't they mostly work to "put down" other groups? Aren't they all based on prejudice—"pre-judging"—rather than personal experience? Many people imagine such stereotypes to be true, but are they really? What do you think? By becoming familiar with them, hopefully we can recognize them in time to stop them before they start.

What are your prejudices? How would you describe the following groups?

Chinese are _____   Blacks are _____

French are _____   Southerners are _____

Foreigners are _____   Mexicans are _____

Asians are _____   Jews are _____

Americans are _____   Hindus are _____

Germans are _____   Russians are _____

Irish are _____   Whites are _____

Native Americans are _____   Arabs are _____

Are there others you have strong stereotypical images of? What are they? Stereotyping creates a simple, general image in the brain. When that stereotyped person or group is encountered, then—click!—the projected image—cheap, dangerous, warlike, greedy— automatically jumps into our minds. Do we stop to question our reaction? No, we usually just assume it is correct and act on it.

***Bigotry** is based on the word "bigot," which refers to one who values only his or her own group, beliefs, race, or political views, and is intolerant of those who differ.*

A bigot has a fixed mind set, an immovable way of thinking that divides completely members of his group from members of another. Bigots think in terms of "my group" vs. "your group." As soon as we have "my" vs. "your" anything, we have conflict. Sectioning the human race into "different" parts is an effect of prejudice that creates separation and conflict.

Discrimination is the act of seeing the difference between one thing or person and another, and making choices based on those differences.

We do this every day. We may choose orange juice over apple juice, a blue pen instead of black, a sitcom instead of the news. You've probably also heard people described as having "discriminating tastes." This means that they care a great deal about their choices, whether in the food they eat, the clothing they wear or the way they live their lives. This kind of discrimination involves making decisions about likes and dislikes and, for the most part, is positive and harms no one.

But what if we discriminate on the basis of opinions that are not true? This is the use of discrimination that creates conflict. In this case, discrimination means making choices based on the wrong stereotypes we carry in our brains. When we have an image in our brains of a certain group as "cheap" or "lazy," and then decide not to make friends with someone or call someone a bad name because he or she belongs to that group, we are practicing discrimination—we are reacting to an individual based on a stereotype of a group that we've been conditioned to believe. The result is easy to predict—conflict inside us that promotes conflict outside us—hostility and discord that can lead to violence.

Scapegoating is making someone bear the blame of others. When a mistake is made or a problem happens, our brain finds someone to blame, to find fault with.

For example, let's say that our Group Y has been conditioned to think that all Group X people are lazy. If we think they are lazy, it is a natural next step to blame them for being lazy, and then to dislike them for this supposed fault. Perhaps we think that because Group X people are lazy, we'll have to do more of the work in the office or factory to make up for them. And if Group X people are lazy, they probably don't even look for work, so they get money from the government, our tax money that we have worked hard to earn. In this case, it is natural for us to be hostile to, or at least disrespectful to, any Group X members. So any member of Group X we run into, we automatically react to negatively—blaming him or her because we have to work harder than we want and don't have as much money as we would like.

Can you see the prejudice in this belief? Can you see how it began as a tiny ant hill and became a mountain? Can you see the effect of this prejudice? It can start with a single, simple "harmless" thought—Group X people are lazy— and escalate into a huge problem for society. This thought, which is certainly not true, can become promoted and professed throughout a country and around the world. The irrational fear that this prejudice can lead to—People of Group X are destroying our economy!—can even lead to the death of millions! Hard to believe? Here's one example:

Throughout the course of history, many groups have blamed Jews for problems in the world and the world's economy. Oddly enough, this has been based on a stereotype of Jews not as being lazy but too "clever with money." In the 1930s, the citizens of Nazi Germany were miserable; their self-respect had been beaten down by the devastation of war and a failed national economy. Their leader, Adolph Hitler, looked for a "scapegoat"— someone they could blame for their own frustration and anger. Adolph Hitler pointed to the Jews and said, "These are the people who are responsible." And the desperate Germans, whose weary brains were very open to conditioning at that time, believed him. Six *million* Jews were killed.

Just as prejudice provides the targets for scapegoating, scapegoating feeds prejudice. It allows us get a problem away from ourselves buy placing it "out there" onto another person or group. This leads us to believe that the solution to the problem is "out there" too, instead of "in here"—within ourselves.

ASK YOURSELF
Are the real roots of prejudice "out there"?
Or are they right here—inside our thoughts?

Our Shadows Continue to Follow Us

The title of this chapter is "The Conditioned Mind is a Dangerous Mind." Can you see how all of these forms of prejudice—stereotyping, bigotry, discrimination, and scapegoating—are dangerous? They all make use of fixed images, conditioned into our brains by those who have gone before us.

We came into a world where many pre-judgments already existed. Without questioning them, our parents, teachers, and friends taught us to think in "old ways," not because they are bad people, but because they were taught these ways by *their* parents—who didn't question them either. We've inherited a huge number of these "names," these "false identities" that really don't match reality. It's as if our brain is full of an encyclopedia of information that is completely wrong. And with wrong information, we make wrong decisions, bad choices.

These old ways are like shadows that follow us. They stay with us and relentlessly cause us to hurt and be hurt, over and over again. At their roots, all forms of prejudice—stereotyping, bigotry, discrimination, and scapegoating—are the same. They're automatic reactions in our brain that result in hurt, anger, and despair. But it is within our power to stop our programmed thinking, and this leads us to our newest discovery.

DISCOVERY 19
Prejudice ends when we can observe it in the making.
Once we observe it, we can stop it in ourselves.

When we see our prejudice, as it's happening, we are engaged in a "Stop! Think!" moment. Our *awareness* of the prejudice stops it, allowing us to pause so that we may examine it; in this moment of clear awareness, we can be free of prejudice.

What follows are more forms of prejudice that are cruel and destructive. As you read about them, allow your awareness of them to help you take a "Stop! Think!" moment to consider what could possibly cause anyone to inflict such harm on other people. While simply knowing about these forms of prejudice cannot right the terrible wrongs they cause, it can help us prevent them from happening in our own lives. If the people involved in these wrongs had understood prejudice better, these things would not have happened.

Racism is the belief that the race we belong to is what defines our character and abilities—who we are and what we can do.

The study of "race" was originally meant to define people in a useful way — to classify us by who we and our ancestors were. To do this scientists study physical characteristics—the color of our hair or eyes, the size and shape of our nose or mouth, bone structure—that make people from one race different from people of another.

I swear...my great, great grandson will avenge me against your great, great...

"Racism," however, uses that information in a negative way. Racism is when we judge others based only on their race, and especially on our stereotyped image on that race. Most often, it is used by one group of people who believe that they are superior to another group. Believing they're better than others allows the self-proclaimed "superior" group to make fun of, or hurt the "inferior" group. In an extreme form, such prejudice can have catastrophic effects.

ASK YOURSELF
Why would someone need to feel better than someone else?
What would I gain by feeling superior to another person?

Slavery *is a system whereby one person actually "owns" another person, and can demand from that person labor or other services.*

In this system a human being is considered property and can be bought and sold. History books tell us that slavery emerged as an "economic necessity of convenience" when people began to establish permanent communities that relied heavily on agriculture. Slavery has been practiced by both primitive and advanced people all over the world, and is thought by many to have ended a hundred and fifty years ago after the American Civil War. In fact, it has been around for many centuries and is still practiced in some parts of the world.

ASK YOURSELF
Do you think slavery emerged simply as an "economic necessity
of convenience"? Or do you think it might have been a good excuse for people to do what they wanted to those they disliked?

In the second century slavery was accepted as legal, despite its being *considered contrary to natural law*. It existed throughout the ancient world, from the Mediterranean regions to China. In Greek cities, a freed slave could not be a citizen, because citizenship was *inherited*. In the fifteenth and sixteenth centuries, European exploration of the African coasts led to a slave trade carried out by the British, French, Dutch, Spanish, and Portuguese. African slaves were in demand on the big farms of the newly discovered Americas, and were brought to Virginia during the seventeenth century.

A movement to abolish slavery for economic and humanitarian reasons began in the eighteenth century. Britain outlawed the slave trade, and Latin American nations abolished slavery when they became independent from Spain in the nineteenth century. Slavery continued, however, in many places, even though it outraged many people's sense of justice.

In the United States, slavery had disappeared in the North by the early nineteenth century, but remained important on the large farms of the South called plantations. The election in 1860 of Abraham Lincoln of the Republican Party, with its anti-slavery platform, led to the secession of Southern states and to the Civil War. Lincoln's Emancipation Proclamation in 1863 and victory by the army of the North ended slavery in the U.S.

ASK YOURSELF
If America was settled by people seeking religious and personal freedom, why was the U.S. one of the last civilized nations to have legal slavery ?

The end of the slavery in America, of course, did not mean the end of discrimination against African-Americans in America. A century later, community activist Rosa Parks refused to leave a bus seat to move to the rear of the bus—which African-Americans were *lawfully required* to do then in Montgomery, Alabama. By forcing the police to remove, arrest, and imprison her, she helped instigate a strong movement in Montgomery that attracted worldwide attention. Activists, teachers, and speakers such as Dr. Martin Luther King, Jr., came to help millions of people to understand the damage that prejudiced minds can cause.

ASK YOURSELF
**People who break the law are considered criminals.
Was Rosa Parks a criminal?**

Although outlawed today in most countries, various forms of slavery still exist. Steps have been taken by international organizations such as the United Nations to curb such practices, but millions of people worldwide still live or work in conditions of slavery.

Genocide *is the deliberate and systematic wiping out of a race, culture, or religious group.*

The word comes from the Greek geno, meaning "related to," and the Latin cida, meaning a "killing." Genocide is a crime against a group. Individuals are victims simply because they belong to the group. In this way, individual members are dehumanized, reduced to numerical statistics.

Although we would like to think of such horrific practices as something that could happen only long ago and far away, in fact, never in the history of the world have so many millions of people been *deliberately* destroyed as during the twentieth century, and mostly in and by so-called "civilized" governments. Societies that have suffered genocide have had at least one significant minority group that was "different" from the majority, usually ethnically, religiously, or politically. Most notorious was Nazi genocide discussed before—the killing of more than six million Jews from all over Europe. The Nazis also killed another six million non-Jews, targeting Gypsies, homosexuals, and Slavs.

Today we ask: How could so many people agree to wiping out another group? The answer is: In the act of genocide, all normal constraints against killing are set aside in the name of a so-called "higher" aim. The reported aim of Adolph Hitler was the "racial purity" of the German people.

ASK YOURSELF
What is "racial purity"?
How could anyone see it as a "higher aim"?

For Stalin in the Soviet Union and Mao Zedong in China, the "higher aim" was economic; millions were killed in order "to build socialism." Other groups of people targeted have been Gypsies and homosexuals, because they were considered "sinful." In Latin America and in the Caribbean areas settled by Spain, millions of Native Indians died in what was regarded as the "march of progress and civilization" led by European Christians. The weaker were displaced in favor of the stronger.

Over the course of the twentieth century, many groups have been in continual opposition: Armenians and Turks, Hindus and Muslims, Serbs and Croats, Irish Protestants and Catholics, Republican and Communist Chinese. In the four years of World War I, more than ten million people were killed.

Millions more were lost in the establishment of Bangladesh in 1971 and the Indochina war ending in 1975. In Cambodia, almost three million people were destroyed by the new Khmer Rouge government for reasons of "economic revitalization."

While it is difficult to even admit that this kind of human behavior has taken place in modern times, our hope is that by looking at these examples, our knowledge and understanding of its causes can help prevent it from happening again.

ASK YOURSELF
Is there any excuse possible for genocide,
for the desire to wipe out an entire group?

Ethnic cleansing is just a polite word for genocide.

Such a term is called a "euphemism," a word that sounds normal and acceptable, but in fact hides a meaning that is really terrible. "Ethnic cleansing" is a term used to describe Serbian treatment of Muslim and Croat minorities (and possible treatment of Serbs by Croats and Muslims). This terrible program was initially undertaken by Serbian forces trying to annex Bosnia and Herzegovina after the breakup of Yugoslavia in the 1990s. The violence was aimed at Muslims, thousands of whom fled the country, while uncounted thousands who remained were killed.

ASK YOURSELF
Consider the phrases "ethnic cleansing" and "genocide."
Which term sounds worse? Which term seems more honest?
Which is more dangerous?

What Prejudice Has Created

What questions can we ask about genocide and ethnic cleansing that can help us understand these inhuman acts? Can we understand why such injustices were able to occur? As human beings who feel this terrible suffering, we want to know:

1. What would cause a group of people to purposely create the deliberate and organized destruction of another group of people?

2. Is it easier to hate, and want to kill, individuals or groups? Which seems less personal?

3. What do you think of these so-called "higher aims" of genocide mentioned? Are any of them good reasons?

4. Do you recall seeing news reports of people fleeing their homeland? Was ethnic cleansing or genocide involved?

5. Were most of these people fleeing guilty of doing something wrong? Or were they innocent?

6. If two factions in one part of the world have been battling for centuries, why do you think they haven't been able to resolve their differences?

Society and Minorities in History

Throughout history we have had minorities. In ancient Greece and Rome, the bulk of work was done by slaves, who were most often from other ethnic groups. Although ethnic groups are probably the most common type of minority group, other minority groups might be based on religion or occupation. During the Middle Ages, there were craft and trade "guilds" that passed their skills from one generation to the next and kept outsiders from getting in. Religious leaders, kings, queens, and nobles had great power; those who raised the food and made the goods everyone needed were at the bottom of society.

India is a country in which some people believe in previous existences. They believe that how we live today depends on how we lived in a previous life. India is also a country with a caste system. A caste is a hereditary group whose members intermarry only among themselves. Each has its own occupations, its own rules relating to kinship, behavior, and even diet. Castes are graded in a social hierarchy in which each expects respect from "inferior" groups and gives respect to "superior" ones.

According to generally accepted beliefs, the caste into which one is born depends on one's *karma*—one's accumulated "good" and "bad" deeds in a previous existence. The way to achieve higher status in future incarnations is to accept one's station in life and live accordingly. There are many castes, but the lowest are the Shudras, who today constitute most of India's artisans and laborers. Below the Shudras are castes with no designations—regarded as "Untouchables" because of their association with unclean occupations. Some scavenge and some clean public toilets with their bare hands. These groups have always been subject to considerable prejudice. The great Indian leader Mohandas K. Gandhi tried to ensure that they were treated humanely and bestowed on them the name Harijan, or children of God, by which they are now popularly known.

While the Indian constitution outlaws "untouchability," and provides each state with special benefits for these people, the Untouchables still exist and continue to do *the work of their ancestors.* Although having one's life dictated by hereditary differences seems obviously unjust, the caste system is regarded by most Hindus as a fair and sensible system. They believe it because that's what they've been conditioned to believe.

ASK YOURSELF
Is it necessary that some group need be at the bottom of society?

The Pecking Order

Have you ever heard of the term "pecking order"? It's a way of life natural to the animal kingdom in which the strongest survive by dominating the weaker. The stronger traits are genetically passed on, to ensure the survival of the species.

In the same way, if one of our tribal ancestors were sick, injured, or too old to work, he or she might be sent away to ensure the safety and comfort of the tribe. Sometimes the weak member was simply sent out to die—a cruel act, but one the tribe deemed necessary for its survival. Survival for our ancestors meant that everyone had to be fit and able to do their job.

Human beings have carried this thinking into modern times, even though the world is vastly different than it was thousands of years ago. Even though they live in security and safety, many people continue to look at the world in terms of a pecking order. They act like members of the primitive tribes, still trying to prove who is most correct, strongest, and best. But today, that way of thinking is more likely to cause trouble than achieve safety. Today, strongly identifying with a "tribe" gets us the *opposite* of what we want, which is to live together in peace.

DISCOVERY 20
Today, fighting to be the most powerful group works against our security. It creates conflict between people and keeps us from acting as a single species.

Minorities today are usually dealt with by the majority in one of two ways: they either become part of the mainstream culture, or they are persecuted. In the process of becoming part of the culture, values and ways of thinking are exchanged and shared between a minority and the majority. Persecution and oppression, on the other hand, separate people and have led to such miserable results as segregation, slavery, and genocide.

What are the potential dangers of prejudice? As we now know, it can lead to the most deadly outcomes imaginable, including the annihilation of millions of people. Think about this the next time you feel like calling someone a bad name.

IN-SIGHTS

★ When we hear words that offend us, it helps to watch our brain for pre-judgments and reactions.

★ In understanding prejudice, it's important to be aware of what words we use and how we use them.

★ Using hurtful words is one way we let our prejudices show.

★ **Stereotyping** is applying a standardized mental picture, held in common by members of a group, that represents an oversimplified opinion, attitude, or judgment.

★ **Bigotry** is based on the word "bigot," which refers to those strongly partial to their own group, beliefs, race, or political views, and is intolerant of those who differ.

★ **Discrimination** is the act of seeing the difference between one thing or person and another, and making choices based on those differences.

★ **Scapegoating** is making someone take the blame for problems caused by others or ourselves.

★ **Slavery** is a system whereby one person owns another and can demand from that person labor or other services. The laborer is considered property, and can bought and sold like merchandise.

★ **Ethnic cleansing** is a polite word used to hide a real act of terror—killing people because they are different.

★ Societies that have suffered genocide have had at least one significant minority group that was "different" from the majority, and easily used as a "scapegoat."

★ Prejudice ends when we can observe it in the making in ourselves.

THINKING FOR YOURSELF

◆ To understand prejudice, do you think it's important to be aware of what words we use in everyday conversation? Why?

◆ Can you see how some thoughts and feelings can lead to words and acts, and therefore lead to conflict?

◆ Can you think of an example of stereotyping that you have done? Is the stereotype shared by your friends or members of your group? Can you see how it is not really true?

◆ Where have you seen signs of bigotry? Do you know someone who's strongly partial to his or her own group and intolerant of anyone who thinks differently? Why do you think bigots are so sure of themselves?

◆ Have you ever discriminated against someone, or some group? What happened? Have you been discriminated against? What was the situation?

◆ When was the last time you made someone a scapegoat? How do you think that made the "scapegoat" feel?

◆ Does it amaze you to know the incredible damage that prejudice can do? Were you aware of this before?

◆ Which form(s) of prejudice have you experienced in your life?

◆ Do you recognize that the real roots of prejudice are exactly where we wish they weren't—inside us all?

Chapter Eight
The Problem With Perfection

Striving for the Ideal

For most of us, the things we believe are hammered into us by our families, and are never questioned. Most of us are brought up to be "good." We may not be *aware* that this "learning to be good" is happening, but it goes on continually. Learning to be good is very important in life, but how we are taught can make a difference in how we see "good."

When I was a child, I didn't know why at the time, but I resisted the way I was being taught to be good. The things I did were judged, by parents or teachers, and it was sometimes painful. I felt bullied when what I did was judged to be "bad," but I also felt bullied when I was judged "good," because I felt *pressured* to act according to what certain authorities in my life said was the right way.

I naturally came to judge myself the same way I was being judged (another example of how we are all conditioned!). I believe this is what made me unhappy in my youth. I was *programmed* to behave in certain ways, and I was *conditioned* to believe that I couldn't know what was right or good myself—that only certain people knew what was right and good and therefore I had to obey them and not listen to what I felt, inside me, was the right thing to do. Even when I did something they judged right, I still didn't feel right.

While the adults in my life meant well, they didn't realize that the way they were teaching me to be good was creating conflict inside me. The conflict I felt was between the **judgment** and the **ideal.** If I did something they considered "bad," they judged me as being less than perfect, and that created conflict in my mind. If I did something they considered "good," I felt they were setting me up to be some kind of ideal or image of perfection they had in their minds, and since I knew I wasn't perfect in any way, *that* created conflict inside me.

Having perfection as an ideal can be, and was for me, destructive. It was something I worked hard at every day, yet something I knew I could never achieve. It was like trying to take a bite of a carrot tied to a string, dangling from a cart that I push in front of me. Every time I moved forward to take a bite, it moved forward, too. Like the carrot, perfection was always just out of reach.

DISCOVERY 21
No one can be perfect.
So trying to be perfect creates conflict.

I felt prejudice because I couldn't live up to the impossible standards that had been set for me. In my mind, they were "they" and I was "I." We were never "we." As a result I felt insecure and continually questioned my personal worth.

While their intention was to make me "good," the attempt to force it to happen caused me to feel less than good. I needed to understand what creates my behavior, who I am, and how I've been conditioned to act in ways that create conflict. I believe I would not have experienced insecurity and doubt of self-worth had I simply been taught to understand how I've been conditioned—how we all think and act in ways that bring about conflict.

DISCOVERY 22
The intelligent way to bring about good behavior
is not through judgment, but through intelligence.

"Of the Blood"

I'm sure you have seen the television program "Star Trek." It's a series of exciting adventures in space exploration. One episode I recall was about something called the "Borg," a collective thing that absorbs everything and everyone into its command. In order for the Borg to feel perfect, it has to make sure that everyone is exactly like it. So, people absorbed into the Borg are like robots—they are logical, but without feeling.

The Borg reminded me of the Nazis of World War II. The Nazi theory of supremacy was based on perfection, which they believed was only possible for the Aryan Race. There was a racial standard, with certain "superior" racial features a person had to have. Anyone not matching up to the standard was excluded, perhaps imprisoned or killed.

At a peace conference in France, a woman from Germany asked where my parents and grandparents came from. When I told her that my mother was German, she said, "Oh, you are of the blood!" Although I said nothing, I thought to myself, "What a prejudiced remark! Do all Germans have a specific kind of blood?"

Adolph Hitler had thousands of followers who became prejudiced like him when they believed everything he told them. He was an authority, their leader, who convinced his people that he had their best intentions at heart. Out of national pride and fear, people followed his instructions and obeyed his rules. Those who didn't were imprisoned or put to death.

When visiting Dachau, a Nazi concentration camp in Germany, long after World War II had ended, I read about the torture and extermination of Jews and others there. People chosen for the camps were selected for one reason: They didn't fit into the Nazi image of "perfect."

Visiting a Nazi concentration camp, I understood the danger of the ideal of "perfection." I began to see that the individuals or groups who established such ideals necessarily created conflict within the human race as a whole. And I began to see that setting up and striving to being perfect, or right, was still going on in the world today. All over the world this idea — that "I" or "my group" represent the right, pure, perfect way, that we are the ones who know and you are the ones who must follow—can lead to violence and suffering.

Our Robotic Nature

Do you remember how the Forgotten Ancestors in the old tribes developed their feelings of security? It was through their realization that there was safety in numbers: I, the individual, am safer with others, the group, than by myself.

This was the beginning of "identification," the need to belong to a group, and keep it together, for self-preservation. Remember how the tribe developed repeated practices — rituals — that were designed to keep the group together, to create a special identity that became more established as customs, traditions, and finally a fully developed culture? And remember how the elements of this culture, the old tribal ways of thinking and acting, were passed down generation after generation from our Forgotten Ancestors to us today?

You and I came into a world already conditioned and prejudiced; we were "socialized," which means that the culture we were born into was programmed into us without question. So, a great deal of what we believe today could be an old tribal inheritance, which we've been conditioned to claim as our legacy. Shouldn't we question any such organized belief systems to find out for ourselves if they are true or false, healthy or destructive? If we don't question the established ways of society, then "authority" can take advantage of us.

The effect of being conditioned with the prejudices of our culture, without questioning them, is that we are acting like robots, mechanical beings, programmed and controlled by someone else.

The Difference Between Conditioning and Educating

There is a huge difference between "conditioning" and "educating," but when we're learning, it can be hard to tell the difference. When we're young, we need intelligent guidance to help us make appropriate decisions. This is education. But sometimes there are "authorities" who believe that they know better than we and want to condition us to accept their beliefs without question.

Some authorities shout slogans, make promises, play stirring music—all to condition us to accept their authority. They want us to vote them into office, or give them money, or support them in their diplomatic games, or even go off to fight and kill their enemies. These dangerous authorities take advantage of us by playing on our conditioning. Prejudiced, we cannot tell who is telling the truth and who isn't, and this prevents us from getting the education we need.

Some authorities will give us healthy and constructive direction, and others will not. It is important that we understand when we are being "educated," shown how to use constructive and intelligent thinking, and when we are being "conditioned," to believe destructive and ignorant thoughts. Understanding the difference is what gives us power.

The Effects of Prejudice

The effects of prejudice are many, and none of them are pleasant. We feel within us irrational fear, anxiety, conflict, and hatred; we respond to others through robotic actions that are cruel and unkind, and cause suffering and conflict that can lead to violence. Above all, we create a world lacking in love and compassion, one in which we are all destined to feel miserable.

If we don't understand prejudice at its roots, and end it *before* it becomes a problem, then we're destined to pass this sad state of affairs on to future generations, the same way it was passed down to us.

ASK YOURSELF
Is ending prejudice something that can wait any longer?

IN-SIGHTS

★ Thinking that what you believe is the only correct way is an act of prejudice. An act of intelligence is asking why we believe what we believe.

★ Conditioning someone to be perfect is not constructive or helpful. Being told we should be perfect can create conflict inside us, causing us to doubt our self-worth because we are not.

★ High standards are admirable, but if we are forced to live up to impossibly high standards, we feel conflict and pain.

★ The Nazi theory of "supremacy" was based on perfection. Anyone not living up to a their standards could be imprisoned or killed.

★ Groups of people who have ideas of "perfection" create conflict within themselves and among the human race. Such views and goals still exist today all over the world.

★ When we're forced to compare ourselves to others, and to see ourselves as "worth-less" than someone else, it is painful and causes us to act in ways we otherwise would never act.

★ The effects of prejudice are many; none are pleasant and some are horrifying.

★ Today, struggling to be the most powerful works *against* our security. It creates conflict and keeps us from acting as a single race.

★ Real power comes from understanding the difference between conditioning and education.

THINKING FOR YOURSELF

✦ Have you been brought up to believe in some established belief system (political, religious, racial)? Do you think you are prejudiced against people who do not share your belief? Have you ever questioned elements of your belief system?

✦ Are you under pressure to meet high standards? Do they inspire you? Do you think any are impossibly high?

✦ Do you think you've ever been conditioned to behave in ways that are harmful? In ways that are helpful? What's the difference?

✦ How do you feel about having to live up to an "ideal"? Is it a good thing? Does it make you feel in conflict? If so, in what way?

✦ What do you think of using modern science to create a "pure" race to be masters of the world? Do you think it is a dangerous idea? Why?

✦ What is your idea of "perfect"? Do you think there are some aspects of perfection that are positive, and some that are negative?

✦ Have you seen evidence of the images of the "ideal" or "perfect" in movies or on television? What were they?

✦ Have you seen a "pecking order" in place anywhere? In what situation?

✦ How does trying to be "the most powerful" work against our security today?

✦ What are some of the effects of prejudice? Do you think we need more evidence that prejudice should be ended as soon as possible?

Chapter Nine
The Anatomy Of Prejudice

How a Prejudiced Bully is Created

What are the qualities of a prejudiced bully? By now, you can probably name quite a few, but like a good scientist, you are withholding judgment until you've gathered all the facts.

A good scientist examines a subject much like a detective at the scene of the crime. A scientist looks for solutions to the problem and works hard not to let emotions rule. A good detective observes the facts of the situation, and from these facts makes certain deductions. With each piece of evidence such a scientific investigator begins to really know what is happening or has happened—as if he or she had firsthand experience.

Here's a challenging project to enhance our understanding of prejudice. Here's where we get to show what we know—and I'm sure we've learned a lot.

Making Our Own Prejudiced Bully

Let's try to find out firsthand what prejudice is by creating a prejudiced bully—in the same way that Dr. Frankenstein constructed his monster. As we put our creature together and consider what we need to do to make him a true bigoted bully, we can review all the ways in which anyone can become a bully.

Let's create this creature from scratch. Pretend that you are a great inventor, and have decided to create this bully—a robot that will deal with people based on its prejudices. Let's call this creature "Zealot." But first, what will our bully be like? Which of the following would best describe him (you can choose from one to three)?

1. Narrow-minded and judgmental
2. Superior and unforgiving
3. Easily influenced by his group

As we have learned, bullies and bigots hold their beliefs strongly, even if they are untrue. Which of the following would be typical of what Zealot believes?

1. Some people are obviously better and more deserving than others
2. People should "stick to their own kind," associate only with their group
3. There can never be true peace in the world

We will be able to tell if we have succeeding in making Zealot a bully by observing how he interacts with other people. Which of the following would describe how we expect Zealot to act? Will Zealot:
1. Ask questions, or follow orders?
2. Prejudge, or find out what someone is really like?
3. Handle a disagreement by fighting, or by reasoning?

Zealot must be able to talk like a bully as well as act like one. Which of the following would we expect to hear Zealot say?
1. "That's the dumbest thing I've ever heard!"
2. "There's only one way to handle that situation!"
3. "People of her kind are always stupid and boring."

Zealot begins life with nothing in its brain. Then, like a computer, we will program him with certain data that he will store in his memory banks. When confronted by a new situation, our prejudiced bully will sort through his memory and decide how to behave. Here are the questions we'll have to answer:
1. How will we turn Zealot into a completely prejudiced bully? What must we do to make Zealot think and act in a bigoted way?
2. Since Zealot will have a computer for a brain, how will we train it, condition it to be prejudiced?
3. What words would you have to teach Zealot to say? What thoughts must Zealot be taught to think? How must Zealot be taught to act?
4. Who should be Zealot's role models? Anyone we know?
5. What would be Zealot's self-image? Someone kind, thoughtful, able to get along well with other people? Or someone critical and easy irritated?
6. Will Zealot believe that he is "better" than other people? Will he be hard to get along with? Will he put down other people?

Now we have an idea of how to begin to create Zealot. Let's begin when Zealot is just developing an awareness of himself in relation to the world.

Training Zealot the Bully

Since Zealot is a robot, he really never has a normal childhood like a human baby. However, the first few weeks of his training—like the formative years of childhood—is when he learns most of the values he will have throughout his "life." Which of the following would be the best sources (you can choose from one to three) to expose Zealot to get him started off in life as a bigot? Think about why you choose what you do. Is it because such sources had the strongest influence on your childhood?

1. Adults who are prejudiced
2. Kids who do whatever "the gang" does
3. TV and printed new stories

We'll need to make Zealot patriotic to one country and flag. And we'll need to brainwash Zealot into believing he must fight to the death in its defense, no matter what the cause or reason. What activity would be best for training "young Zealot" to be this way?

1. Watching war movies
2. Listening to political speeches
3. Reading "action hero" comic books

Zealot will want to make fun of people because they look, dress, or speak "funny." He will need to learn mean and hurtful ways to put people down. What would be the best source for this training?

1. Comedy club routines
2. Political debates
3. Arguments between adults

Zealot will need to be taught to be tough and violent and how to fight and kill. What would be a good activity for teaching him these skills?

1. Playing video games
2. Joining a sports team
3. Watching violent movies

Choosing some "role models" for Zealot should help him develop good bully characteristics. Who of the following do you think should be Zealot's heroes?

1. Movie action heroes
2. Pro wrestlers
3. Big business tycoons

Perhaps "young Zealot" would learn faster if he had some appropriate toys to play with. Which of these would be best for helping him learn the message of bigotry you are trying to teach him?
1. Action figures
2. Racing cars
3. Video games

Finally, let's look at some "advanced training" to Zealot. Which of the following might we do to him to make sure he becomes a really "great" bully:
1. Beat him up occasionally, for no reason
2. Constantly call him names, like "you stupid robot"
3. Laugh at everything he does, because he's not even human

By now you have noticed that there are no wrong answers to the questions above; all these people and activities may be sources of prejudiced attitudes. The reason we've chosen them to help condition "young Zealot" is because we now understand how they have conditioned our own brains.

But let's look at the other side of this question. Are there any activities we would *not* want Zealot to do, because we would be afraid they might keep him from becoming prejudiced? What "dangerous" activities should Zealot *not* be allowed to do?
1. Read a great work of literature from another country
2. Volunteer to work in a homeless shelter
3. Help friends who are having trouble with their schoolwork
4. Raise money for a local charity
5. Correspond with a "pen pal" in another country
6. Visit a local art museum
7. Spend a semester abroad as an exchange student
8. Start a club for anyone interested in drawing or painting
9. Write to a local newspaper about something wrong or unfair
10. Try the food of another country for the first time

Again, there are no wrong answers. If we were trying to train Zealot to be the perfect robot bully, we would not want him to do any of the above activities. But why? How might some of these activities work to make Zealot less prejudiced, less of a bully? What if everybody engaged in activities like these on a regular basis? Can we imagine a world in which there are fewer prejudiced people? If we can make prejudiced bullies like Zealot, can we unmake them?

DISCOVERY 23
Without prejudiced people, there can be no prejudice.

Zealot, the Bully, Exists!

Creating our bully, Zealot, has been an exercise of the imagination, but we have learned a lot. And we know that there is no need to really create such a creature, even if we could, because there are enough Zealots in the world already. In fact, since we have all been conditioned by the same people and sources that we would have used to train Zealot, we can say that we all have a little bit of Zealot inside us.

ASK YOURSELF
What causes prejudice—education or conditioning?

The following may sound like a puzzle, but in fact it's just a statement that happens to be true. Think about it and you will come to understand it:

When we think hard about *making* peace, we create conflict.
But when we get rid of all that prevents peace, peace comes naturally.

In other words, attempting to live according to a peaceful ideal—setting a goal of thinking only peaceful thoughts and acting only in peaceful ways—creates conflict inside us, because it leads us judge ourselves and others as "bad" for having non-peaceful thoughts or engaging in non-peaceful acts. But eliminating such unrealistic goals that prevent peace *gives* us peace.

IN-SIGHTS

★ By "building" a prejudiced bully ourselves, we get firsthand experience in how and why a bully thinks and acts as he does.

★ Our "perfect" robot bully, Zealot, will be bigoted, judgmental, and unforgiving.

★ Zealot will use language that makes him feel superior and other people feel uncomfortable.

★ Our prejudiced robot bully, like a child, must be "conditioned" by exposure to prejudiced information and opinions, through adults, friends, TV, and the movies.

★ From people who use critical and hurtful words, Zealot will learn how to put people down and make fun of them because of how they look, dress or speak.

★ From patriotic people, Zealot will learn why his country is always "right," and become convinced he should fight and die for it.

★ From people who are engaged in violent activities, Zealot will learn how to fight, hurt, and even kill others.

★ Zealot will always turn to violence as the obvious way to resolve a disagreement.

★ Without prejudiced people, there can be no prejudice.

★ If we know how to make a Zealot, a prejudiced bully, we should know also how to *unmake* him.

★ Setting a goal of thinking only peaceful thoughts and acting only in peaceful ways creates conflict inside us, because it leads us judge ourselves and others as "bad" for having non-peaceful thoughts or engaging in non-peaceful acts.

114

THINKING FOR YOURSELF

◆ Are bullies born bullies or are they "built" through conditioning?

◆ As you were building your prejudiced bully, were all the choices you were given easy to make?

◆ Did having firsthand experience in building a bully help you see what turns a person into a bully?

◆ Do you think you were taught the way Zealot was taught? Do you see any of Zealot's characteristics in yourself?

◆ What kind of training do you think prejudiced bullies get that perhaps you and I didn't get?

◆ How do you think bullies get to be tough, angry, and violent?

◆ Do you think most bullies might have been victims who use bullying as a way to protect themselves?

◆ Can you tell bullies by the language they use? Think of an example of something you can say in a nice way, then say the same thing in a mean and hurtful way.

◆ Now that you've had the experience of building Zealot, does he remind you of anyone you've ever read about in history or in the news? Who?

◆ Everyone of us has a little bit of Zealot inside. What activities might help us *unmake* our prejudices?

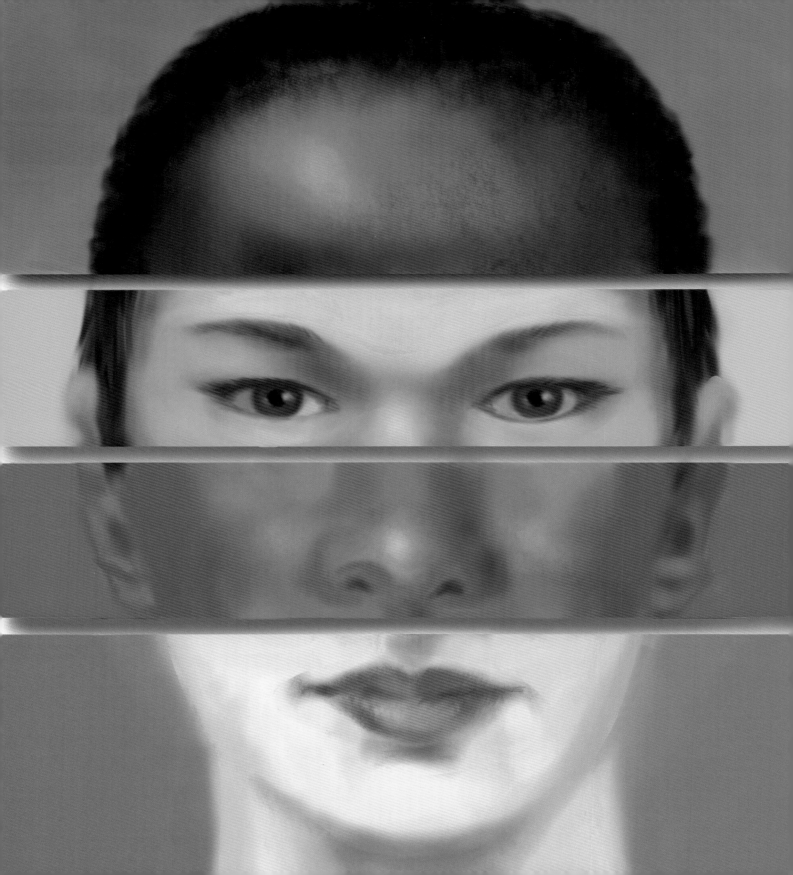

Can We Get Free of Our Prejudice?

Chapter Ten
Taking Time to Stop

Insight Makes Us Free

Several students were gathered around their teacher. The class had been discussing prejudice for some time now, and the teacher wanted to be sure that her students knew exactly what it was.

The teacher said to her students, "I want you to show me prejudice. What does it look like? How do you know when you're seeing it? If you can recognize it, then you can show it to me."

The students looked puzzled. One raised her hand.

"Prejudice is bullying someone because his skin is a different color than yours," she said.

A boy raised his hand. "Prejudice is not liking another group because they speak a foreign language that you don't understand," said the boy behind her.

Another student said, "Prejudice is thinking that you and your friends are superior to other people."

The teacher said, "What you've all given me are words. I want someone to *show* me prejudice—without using a single word."

Just then Mariko, a Japanese-American student, raised her hand and, when motioned by the teacher, got up and went to the front of the room. On the teacher's desk was a holder with small flags sticking out, each from a different country. Mariko chose the flag of Japan for herself. Motioning two other students to come forward, she gave the British flag to Thomas, a student from England, and a the flag of Mexico to Juanita, whose parents had come from that country.

Then, suddenly raising her Japanese flag above her head, she stuck out her tongue and made a face at Thomas and Juanita. Juanita began to smile, but Thomas got angry, raised his flag even higher than Mariko's, and stuck his tongue out at her as well. When Juanita saw this she joined in, raising her flag high and made a face at both of the others.

Soon, all three students were reaching as high as they could in order to make their flag the top one, and making mean faces and gestures at each other. The class was shocked. When Juanita stood on a chair to make her flag higher, Thomas climbed on top of a desk.

The teacher applauded, as did the other students. She thanked Mariko for her help and explained, "The response of each of you before Mariko was not wrong, but those were *verbal examples* that you had learned and remembered. Mariko *showed* us prejudice. She gave us an example and even an experience of prejudice. She showed us how easy it is to see ourselves as separate from one another and, therefore, how easily conflict is created.

"Words have a place. An explanation of prejudice is the first step toward understanding, but we must go further. Explanations help us understand a problem, but cannot help us solve the problem. By themselves, sometimes they can create more conflict. We have to go deeper.

"Mariko showed us that we can *see* prejudice—that we can recognize it happening in the moment. Is that a good thing, do you think? Why would it be a good thing to be able to recognize prejudice the moment it happens?"

Thomas raised his hand. "If you can see it happen—in that moment maybe you can stop it."

"How do you mean, Thomas?" the teacher asked.

"The second you see prejudice happening, you can stop and you can think: 'This is an act of prejudice. Am I going to participate in it, or not?'"

"Yes!" said Juanita. "By recognizing prejudice, it's almost as if you have come to the fork in a road. You can go right, or you can go left."

Nelson, whose family was from Africa, was nodding his head. "You can jump onto Prejudice Road by judging, or you can take Sherlock Holmes Road and question."

"And by questioning, you begin to see what you've got!" said Thomas.

"Thank you, students," the teacher said. "You have shown me that you can see prejudice, and you have gained insight."

The Art of In-Sight

In the example I just related, Mariko got the other students to see how they were separating themselves from one another and, therefore, creating conflict. So, the question is: Can an explanation end prejudice? Or, can prejudice end only when we're actually *aware* of it, as it's happening—while we're experiencing it?

The fact is, an explanation is a description. Most people think they understand prejudice because they've memorized a description—the words—and they look for answers or solutions to this problem called prejudice. But there is no "solution" that can come from thinking alone; "thinking about" solutions to prejudice is not "doing."

The real discovery of what prejudice is comes in the experiencing of it, seeing it as it occurs in the brain. "Aha! I just made a prejudiced remark!" This is insight—seeing *in*. Spotting prejudice, right when it happens, is real information, and therein lies the opportunity to end it. That's what we're going to look at now, and I know you're ready to take this exciting step.

But, don't forget! You must discover all of this for yourself. You need to question what I tell you. Otherwise, how will you know whether or not it's true?

Inner Imaging

Prejudice is often born quietly—sometimes without us noticing. It begins like a headache and, before we know it, our whole body is aching. We have caught a disease and we can't seem to shake it. We can prevent prejudice by keeping in mind one basic question whenever we feel a "prejudice attack" coming on: "Am I questioning, or am I judging?"

It is natural for human beings to offer their "educated" ideas to others. When people learn something they believe is important, they're usually anxious to pass it on. Someone may try to convince us that a particular conflict is being fought because of actions of one side, while someone else may be trying to show us how the fighting was started by the *other* side. How do we know for ourselves what to believe?

DISCOVERY 24
**We believe what we've been either *educated* or *conditioned* to believe.
Education brings us understanding; conditioning brings us prejudice.**

All of us have had the experience of going to a doctor or dentist to get an X-ray. It's amazing that such imaging machines can show us what's going on *inside* our bodies, things that we cannot see. We need to develop a *mental* imaging machine that does something similar—one that helps us detect prejudice when we cannot see it.

A.R.M.ing Ourselves to Deal with Prejudice

Below is a simple organization scheme, which we call A.R.M., to help us look at the three main levels at which we deal with conflict arising from prejudice.

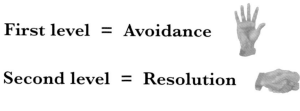

First level = Avoidance

Second level = Resolution

Third level = Management

Avoidance: Stopping the Act of Prejudice

The first level occurs at the root of the feeling. The moment we witness prejudice, we catch it in the act and we **avoid** it—by stopping it *before* it starts.

For example, suppose someone calls you a terrible name. Your natural reaction is to call that person a bad name in return. But instead—to stop conflict before it starts—you take a Stop! Think! moment. Then, you walk away. Or make a joke about it. Or say, "Why did you call me that name? Are you angry about something? What's wrong?"

Is this the exact opposite action you want to take? Do you think it's difficult to *act* this way instead of *react* to the name you were called? Are you thinking, "No way am I going to let that person get away with that!"?

That's understandable. But here's the point: You can choose to stop prejudice in its tracks, by not participating in the act of prejudice. In doing so you stop conflict—not only in your mind, but between you and that person. This is a new way of thinking that confers amazing power on all who can master it!

If you've ever been in a car that's about to hit a wall, and someone steps on the brake just in time—you know what it means to *prevent* something from happening. Braking in time, you are able to prevent a crash that would have occurred.

Imagine that wall to be the Wall of Conflict, and you see how the level of avoidance works. By recognizing instantly that you are acting out of prejudice, you step on the brake and keep yourself from hitting that wall—preventing a crash into conflict.

Resolution: Resolving the Conflict Created by Prejudice Now

The second level is reached when prejudice has already become a problem and is already creating conflict. In order to end the prejudice that is causing the conflict at this level, we have to **resolve** it. It's too late to prevent it, but we can find a way to end it as soon as possible.

For example, suppose someone calls you a name and you—unable to walk away, unable to joke about it, unable to stop yourself—call a name back. The conflict has begun between you and the other person because there are differences between you that need to be resolved.

Although this has happened before, this time, you see it! You realize that you made the mistake of calling that person a name, too, and you understand, after the fact, that you still have the power, right now, to stop the conflict from intensifying.

So, when the person calls you another name or angrily walks up to you—this time, you try to talk it out. You say, "This name-calling stuff doesn't work for me. There has to be a better way to work this out. Let's talk about it." You stop the bullying by using mental self-defense.

DISCOVERY 25
Instead of fighting, we can reason with a bully.
We can use our brain instead of our fists.

Learning how to **resolve** can be great fun! It makes you feel powerful because your brain does the work instead of your body! Here are twelve ways to walk away with confidence that will help you resolve conflict non-violently.

Twelve Ways to Walk Away With Confidence

1. **Make friends.** Treat the bully as a friend instead of an enemy.
2. **Use humor.** Turn a threatening situation into a funny one.
3. **Walk away.** Don't get into it, just walk away.
4. **Use cleverness.** Use your imagination to resolve the conflict.
5. **Agree with bully.** Let insults go without fighting back.
6. **Refuse to fight.** The winner of a fight is the one who avoids it.
7. **Stand up to bully.** Stick up for yourself. Just say NO! to bullying.
8. **Yell!** A powerful shout can end conflict before it starts.
9. **Ignore the threat.** Like bamboo, bend in the wind.
10. **Use authority.** Call a teacher or adult to help you end the conflict.
11. **Reason with bully.** Use the most powerful tool you have—your brain.
12. **Take a martial arts stance.** When all else fails, be a victor, not a victim.

Management: Containing the Conflict Caused by Prejudice

The third level is arrived at when conflict created by prejudice is inevitable. It's too late to avoid it. It's too late to resolve it. All you can do is **manage** it. Managing is simply "keeping the lid on."

For example, two of you have called each other names, and you've begun to fight, and it now seems impossible to stop until one of you is knocked out. Your head is bleeding, and the other person's glasses are broken. You can still hold up your hands and say, "Enough! this is getting out of hand." Or you can walk away. Or you can call for help. Or you can choose *not* to hurt your opponent any more than necessary to get away.

The point is, you still have choices.

It's when you don't make the right choices—or don't know you have any choices—that conflict can get out of hand. This is the kind of uncontrolled conflict we see when racial, cultural, or national groups war over their beliefs—such as what has happened in Rwanda, Bosnia, Northern Ireland, South Africa, the Middle East, among others.

These are situations in which hatred and bigotry have carried people away to levels of conflict that seems unbelievable to us. But it's important to realize that such acts are not just something that happens "over there" by "those people." Perhaps we should remember that American soldiers were court-martialed for killing innocent Vietnamese in the village of Mi Lai during the Vietnam War. We should remember the Ku Klux Klan, gangs of white people who beat and killed African-Americans, right here in the USA. It's not that we wish to re-live horrifying incidents in human history, but we must remember: All human beings—including ourselves—are capable of joining in the uncontrolled conflict that our prejudices can cause.

ASK YOURSELF
Why do we wait until it's too late—until we have to *manage* conflict?
Wouldn't it be easier to *avoid* or *resolve* it?

Taking Responsibility

Whether prejudice has led us to problems at the first, second or third levels, the most important thing you can do is understand the cause or root of it. To do this you must first take responsibility. You must say to yourself: "I have somehow been a part of creating this problem."

Whether you have or not at this point doesn't make any difference. What is important is that you accept responsibility. Only then is it possible to honestly say to yourself: "Since I may have taken part in creating the problem, let me think of some way I might be helpful in resolving it."

If we can **manage** it now, perhaps we can **resolve** it next time by changing our response. If we can *resolve* it now, perhaps we can **avoid** it next time by changing our response. In any case, we need to go to the first stage and educate ourselves about the causes of this conflict, so that next time, we can end it at the root level.

Intellectual Understanding or Real Insight?

Stopping conflict at the first stage—by avoiding it—shows **insight**. This is the ability to recognize conflict, or even potential conflict arising from prejudice, right now, as it is happening, so that it can be stopped immediately. Since insight allows us to stop conflict at this first stage, attaining it always our highest goal.

Stopping conflict at the second stage—by resolving it— shows **hindsight.** Yes, unfortunately, there was conflict. Yes, I see that what that person did was an act of prejudice, and what I did was a reaction to that prejudice. Still, ending conflict at the second stage, through hindsight, shows an understanding that prejudice created conflict.

Stopping conflict only at the third stage—through managing it—we might call **"late sight,"** because we're too far gone to stop or undo what created it. It is a sign that we have an intellectual understanding that conflict took place, but that we were helpless to prevent it. There's no time to do anything about it now except to go about the business of cleaning up the mess, repairing the damage, and getting on with our lives.

But what about next time? Can we do better? As with any activity, practice makes for better skills. As we practice and get better at X-raying our thoughts, our ability to stop conflict arising through prejudice more quickly will improve.

> ## DISCOVERY 26
> **No matter what level it gets to,**
> **prejudice needs to be stopped in its tracks,**
> **before it rises to the next level.**

Choosing Responsibility over Blame

As we've learned, one of the most valuable tools in our search for understanding is questioning. When we question, we can find out for ourselves whether something is true or false. Hopefully, what you've read in this book is true, because it has been our intent to say only what's true. But how will you be sure?

A scientist gathers and observes facts, and from those facts deduces or creates insights. Insight is being able to clearly see what's happening as it occurs. It's firsthand experience, rather than something someone tells you. What is necessary in understanding and ending prejudice is not memorizing information about it, but seeing what prejudice actually is through your own observation.

By questioning, we become more objective, more fair. We can look at the problem, see it for what it is and accept responsibility for taking part in its avoidance, resolution or management.

DISCOVERY 27
No one is to blame.
I must take responsibility for my own life.

In order to understand how our thinking became conditioned, we have to take action—become active in our own education. We can speak with people we know. But all anyone can do is tell us something or show us something. It's then up to us to find out for ourselves whether what we've been told or shown is true or not. That is real education, and only real education ends prejudice.

IN-SIGHTS

★ It's natural for people to offer their "educated ideas" to others. When we learn something we believe is important, we like to pass it on. But before we do, we need to find out whether what we believe is true.

★ We believe what we've been conditioned to believe which, sometimes, is how we become prejudiced.

★ Thanks to X-rays and other imaging machines, we can see what physically goes on inside our bodies. In the same way, we need a *mental* imaging machine—one that helps us detect prejudice inside us.

★ There are various levels at which we humans deal with conflict arising from prejudice:
        Avoidance—Stop it before it starts
        Resolution—Resolve it now
        Management—Contain it as much as possible

★ By stopping prejudice in its tracks, we stop conflict—not only in our own minds, but between ourselves and another person.

★ Learning to stop conflict in its tracks makes us feel powerful, because our brain does the work instead of our body.

★ Most of us pay no attention to conflict until it's too late. Rather than avoid or resolve it, we let it go until we're forced to manage it.

★ As we practice and get better at X-raying our thoughts, we can stop prejudice more quickly, and so stop conflict before it gets out of hand.

★ One way to get free from prejudice is to make sure that we're being properly educated instead of conditioned.

THINKING FOR YOURSELF

◆ When was the last time you witnessed prejudice as it was happening? Do you remember the situation? Did you manage to avoid it?

◆ How do you feel about not calling someone a name back, after that person has called you a name? Do you think you can do it?

◆ What do you think are the benefits of not reacting, but instead acting in your own behalf by not calling someone a name back?

◆ Do you understand that prejudice is best solved at the first level, by recognizing it and avoiding it?

◆ Resolving or managing prejudice is far more difficult than nipping it in the bud. But if you had no choice, do you think it can be stopped at these stages? How?

◆ Do you think that working out details for fixing a problem is at least better than doing nothing at all? Have you been in a situation where the resolution seemed hopeless? What did you do?

◆ Why do you think we wait until it's too late to pay attention to most conflicts? Wouldn't it be easier to avoid them or resolve them?

◆ What do you think are the benefits of learning to reason with a bully with your brain instead of your fists?

◆ Which is easier—to take responsibility for a bad situation or to blame someone else? Which is the best way if our goal is to end prejudice? Which will lead to better control over a similar situation in the future?

Chapter Eleven

Prejudice Is A Decision

The Innocent: A Story

A young man was kept in a dark cellar and chained in a harness to a large, rusted ring attached to the stone floor. He had been there all eighteen years of his life. His only distraction was a wooden horse, a toy he played with. As he moved the wooden toy back and forth on the stone ground, he spoke only one word, "Horse." He lived and slept in darkness, until that day when the man in the dark hat and robe came.

The man unlocked the heavy door and entered the darkness. He walked over to the young man and bent down to unlock the chain. The young man paid no attention to what was happening. The older man picked up the young man, who had never before stood up. He held the young man, then lifted him onto his back and carried him out of the dark chamber into the brilliant light of day.

The older man placed the young man on the ground. The young man lay blinking at the unfamiliar day. The older man then dressed the younger man in new clothes. Then the older man stood the young man up and held him from behind. In order to get him to walk, the older man kicked the young man's booted heels from behind. Step by step, the old man, holding the young man from behind, moved forward.

He then placed the young man in a horse-drawn cart that was waiting nearby. The young man lay in the back staring wide-eyed at the world passing him by as the older man guided the cart down the hillside, urging the horse to move faster and faster.

Soon they approached the outskirts of a town. The older man lifted the young man out of the cart and, kicking at his heels, got him to walk to the center of the town square. It was early in the morning and the townspeople were still asleep. The older man put a rolled piece of paper in the young man's hand and left him standing alone in the square, then quickly retreated to his cart, and dashed over the hill and out of sight.

At sunrise, the townspeople awoke. Outside, standing completely still in the town square, the young man waited—for what, he didn't know. Soon people came out of their houses and, upon seeing the young man standing so still with a paper clenched in his outstretched hand, they began to inquire about who he was. But they got no answer because the young man could not speak. In fact, he knew nothing except that dark chamber and his little wooden horse. He had never seen anything of the world outside his prison. He was completely innocent, like a newborn baby, except that he was eighteen years old.

This is a true story about a young man named Kasper Hauser, a name that was written on the paper he clenched in his hand when he was found, in the early 1800s. The people who lived in this small town in Germany did not know what to do with him, so they locked him up in one of their jail cells, until a professor found him, took him home and cared for him the rest of his life.

Kasper would often fall into a deep sleep from which he could not be awakened. People thought that he was retarded and felt sorry for him, but there was nothing wrong with him. He was completely normal, except for the fact that he had never seen *anything* outside the dark stone chamber where he'd lived for eighteen years.

Kasper was completely unprejudiced. He had no preconceptions or ideas about anything. His mind was a clean slate. He'd never seen light before and when he first saw a candle, he tried to pinch the flames with his fingers, shocked to suddenly experience pain.

Can you imagine what it would be like to be eighteen years old and never have experienced anything but darkness? No light, no people, no birds, trees, sky, flowers, no smell of spring, no sensation of talking or laughing or singing or crying. Nothing! He was a newborn in a man's body.

Looking Through Kasper Hauser's Eyes

A fascinating fact is that Kasper Hauser had no prejudices—none. He didn't know how to discriminate between a black person and a white person. He'd never been taught to feel superior to other people, to call anyone names, to feel jealousy, spite, hatred, or even fear. His life proved something important.

DISCOVERY 28
Prejudice is not something we're born with.
It's something we learn.

Prejudice is not natural to human beings. If people have no preconceived images of themselves and therefore of others, then prejudice cannot exist. The roots of prejudice take hold in the human brain according to how that brain is trained to think and feel.

One way to free ourselves of prejudice is to look at the world through Kasper Hauser's eyes. Look at a tree as if you've never seen one before. What do you notice first? Get a whiff of an apple pie as if you'd never smelled one before. How would you describe the scent? The next time you hear music, respond to it as if you'd never before heard a melody. What words come to mind? And the next time you see people whose skin color is different, or who speak with an accent, or who dress uniquely—how does it feel to take in the wonder of their difference?

Looking at Our "Automatic" Reactions

Years ago, high schools began to offer drivers' education courses to help students learn how to drive a car safely. One of the activities was to be able to stop quickly for a red light. Students were "conditioned" to learn to stop for that light for a very good reason—safety. Therefore, it was a positive, constructive form of conditioning.

In class was a machine that would blink red, and students had to quickly move their feet from the fake gas pedal to the fake brake pedal. Reactions were timed to see how fast students could move.

For those of us who learned to drive that way and who have been driving for many years, that action has been performed thousands of times, for real. And thankfully, it has worked and kept us safe.

On older cars, drivers were conditioned to "pump" the brakes—push down and let go several times— to stop the car. We were warned that if we "slammed on" the brakes—pushed once, hard and fast—we would "lock up" the brakes and skid out of control. So we practiced pumping until it became an automatic response. New cars now have something completely different, called ABS (for "automatic braking system"). With this new system, drivers are told *not* to pump the brakes. Instead, we're supposed to push down once, hard, and hold our foot there.

Looking at this automotive improvement objectively, it certainly appears to me that pushing down hard once is easier than pumping the brakes. The problem is, this pushing-down-once action makes no sense to my body, which has been conditioned for all these years to pump. So the first time I started to skid on ice with the ABS system in my car, I pumped — and kept on skidding. I couldn't override my body's conditioned reaction. It had been reinforced for so long that it was an automatic response in me. My brain went on "automatic" when I started to skid. I had to practice on ice with the new ABS system repeatedly to "de-condition" myself not to react in the old way.

That's how it is with prejudice. Instead of giving in to our "automatic" reaction, we need to become aware that the old way doesn't work. This awareness should create a "Stop! Think!" moment that allows new thinking to take place. Then we can act in a new way.

Although getting accustomed to brakes and becoming prejudiced both come from conditioning and habit, a major difference between them is that one is constructive and the other is destructive. We want to become aware that the old way isn't working, so we can appropriately respond to the new ABS braking system. But we don't want to free ourselves from one type of prejudice only to be conditioned into a new one—particularly in relation to people. Brakes on cars are one thing; our relationships with other humans is another.

We're all vulnerable to the effects of prejudice, but we're all also capable of understanding how we've been conditioned and responding correctly to a new situation. Here are three steps that can help:

1. **Become aware** of new information we need.
2. **Concentrate** on what is new that we need to do.
3. **Focus** on the new way until we understand it.

First, we must *become aware of new information we need.* Any action we take that is not based on awareness is really a reaction. Whether we react to a red light or to someone who is different from us, our reaction is mechanical unless we make ourselves aware of what is happening. That awareness will give us information we didn't have before, and will affect the way we think about a particular situation.

Next, we must *concentrate on what is new that we need to do*. Once we're aware, we stop the reaction in its tracks! We're ready to act instead of react. In that Stop! Think! moment, we can ask:

Is this a conditioned action?

Is it constructive, or destructive?

Is my *new* behavior based on prejudice, too?

Is my mind's door open to new information?

Does my mental X-ray machine show judgment, or understanding?

Finally, we must *focus on the new way until we understand it*. We must focus regularly and often on our new way of thinking and behaving. The way we became conditioned in the first place was the result of time and repetition; now we must focus our attention on how that conditioning works inside us. When we're aware of what's happening both inside and outside us, we learn new behavior just by keeping our mind open to new possibilities.

We must never be afraid to stop in the middle of actions or thoughts that could prove destructive—to ourselves or others.

IN-SIGHTS

★ Prejudice is not something we're born with.

★ The strange life of Kasper Hauser proves that someone who is prejudiced must have *learned* those prejudices.

★ If people have no preconceived images of themselves and of others, prejudice cannot exist.

★ The roots of prejudice grow in the human brain according to how it is conditioned to think and feel.

★ Although we are born innocent, we're born into a world already infected with prejudice, so it is only a matter of time before we catch it ourselves.

★ While we're all vulnerable to the effects of prejudice, we can free ourselves from conditioned thinking and action.

★ Three steps that can help break out of our conditioned ways of thinking and acting:
   1. **Become aware** of new information we need.
   2. **Concentrate** on what is new that we need to do.
   3. **Focus** on the new way until we understand it.

★ The way we became conditioned in the first place took time and repetition. Developing new patterns of thought and behavior will take time and practice as well.

★ Prejudice is a conditioned attitude. We can free ourselves of the hatred that prejudice creates by paying attention to its root causes.

★ We must never be afraid to stop in the middle of actions or thoughts that could prove destructive to ourselves or others.

THINKING FOR YOURSELF

✦ What does the story of Kasper Hauser mean to you? Can we learn anything from it?

✦ Can you imagine what it must be like to be eighteen years old and never have experienced anything but darkness and a single toy?

✦ Why do you think Kasper Hauser had no prejudices? Do you think his early life proves that any person who is prejudiced had to have learned those prejudices?

✦ Do you think anyone who bullies another person for being different is *taught* to do this? By whom? For what reason?

✦ If prejudice is not natural to human beings, why do you think so many people are prejudiced and act in prejudiced ways? Are we all vulnerable to the effects of prejudice? Is there anyone who is not?

✦ Why do you think it's important to concentrate on what's new that you need to do? Why is focusing on your new way of doing things so important?

✦ We re-arrange our furniture, we re-condition our cars, and we re-novate old buildings. Does it make sense that we can to re-condition our thinking and behavior?

✦ Do you think attempting to re-condition our thoughts and actions only creates more problems, more conflict? Why?

✦ We've discussed ways to change our own conditioned thinking. How might we go about doing that in our homes, schools, and communities?

Chapter Twelve
Thinking In New Ways

A Right-Side-Up World

A young girl named Jean had a dream. She dreamed that we all lived in a world where everything was right-side up. This world was a place where children played with one another and didn't fight. Adults weren't too busy to play with their children when they got home from work, and couldn't wait to spend time with each other. In her dream world, being a schoolteacher was the most respected job and, therefore, the most highly paid. Television programs showed kind people who loved to learn and have fun. Movies were exciting and adventuresome without people killing one another.

In Jean's dream, her brother and sister had the same kind of job and earned the same income. Her father helped with the dishes and helped clean up on weekends, and her mother, a skilled carpenter, built an addition to their house. And one of her favorite parts of the dream was that her brother, after inviting her to play basketball with him, sat and talked with her about things he likes. They talked about how all the people they knew cooperated with one another and how great it was that in their world there was no conflict.

In the right-side-up world there were no poor people and there were no people with so much money that they didn't know what to do with it. Everyone finally figured out that there's just so much to go around, and everybody got a fair and equal share of everything there was to be had—whether homes, toys, friends, and love.

In Jean's dream, nobody had to be taught how to be "good," and nobody was "bad." Being happy meant living intelligently, honestly, and peacefully. There were no soldiers and no wars, because people understood what created conflict and how to avoid it. As a result, there were no lawyers, no judges, and no prisons.

It was a lovely dream, but the dawn came, and Jean woke up.

As we all know, the world we live in is different from the one in Jean's dream. We live in a world in which prejudices run through our daily lives and have effects on us that we're only beginning to recognize.

Did you know that the country of Costa Rica, in Central America, has no army? And did you know that all the money that could have been spent on the military goes toward education? Isn't this is a little bit like Jean's right-side-up world? Does this help you realize that such a world might possible?

For you and me, slowly the gray-colored glasses that sit on our noses have started to slip off. We're beginning to see the world in a new light, like Kasper Hauser, and we're grasping new insights—learning how to brake as fast as we can to avoid conflict.

Pulling Out the Roots of Prejudice

After reading this book, you no longer are able only to *imagine* prejudice as a concept. What you are able to do now is to *perceive* prejudice—to see it in action, right as it's happening—which enables you to stop it instantly. In case you doubt your ability, here's a brain science project designed to pull the roots of prejudice from your brain, once and for all.

As you've already learned, your brain has been programmed with misinformation that can cause prejudice and lead to panic and conflict. Your task as a Brain Scientist is to recognize this computer error and restructure the brain with correct and accurate responses that will undo conditioned programming and lead to understanding and well-being. The chart and directions that follow will give you the in-sights needed to correct this problem.

The World is Upside Down

Can there be a balance?

WAYS OF APPROACHING AN
UNKNOWN PERSON, GROUP, OR THING

PATH TO CONFLICT

↓

CONDITIONED RESPONSE

1. A conditioned image appears in the brain
2. The image provokes conditioned thoughts and feelings.
3. Pre-judgment (=prejudice) takes place.
4. Conclusion: This situation is dangerous!

↓

Threat ⇒ **Fear**

FIGHT OR FLEE!

↓

Feeling of panic

↓

Need to defend

↓

CONFLICT

STOP! THINK!

PATH OF PEACE

↓

INTELLIGENT QUESTIONING

1. I have heard something about this, but is it true?
2. Do I have to think this way?
3. I will look at all the evidence myself.
4. Conclusion: I see nothing bad or dangerous here.

↓

No Threat ⇒ **Calm**

RELAX AND ENJOY

↓

Feeling of confidence

↓

Desire to resolve

↓

PEACE

Fact: When you have a conditioned response, your brain is doing what it should do, preparing you to deal with a threat. But in the above case, the threat is imagined. You are receiving mistaken information—thoughts and feelings of fear and danger—due to false programming, conditioning. This false information puts you on a Path to Conflict.

The key is to Stop! Think! and check your thoughts. Don't be afraid of these thoughts—they are only thoughts. They cannot hurt you. Don't run away from them. Stay with them and learn about how you've been conditioned to think this way. Ask yourself: Is this information I've just received true, or false? Do I have all the information I need to make an intelligent decision? Did I get the facts, or did I get someone's else's wrong opinions? We are directed down the Path to Conflict by "false self-talk" which is mental programming, or prejudice. When we experience false self-talk, it's important to:

Remember that the brain doesn't know the difference between an imagined threat or a real one. It reacts as if the imagined threat is real.
Be aware that those false thoughts create anxiety and fear, and can lead to conflict.
Understand that those false thoughts are learned, and can be unlearned.
Know that every thought has its own chemistry. We feel what we think.
Stop your old, conditioned way of thinking by seeing the falseness of it.
Examine the facts and replace false information with truthful statements.

Clue: When you start down the Path to Conflict, imagine a big, red STOP sign in your mind to stop your conditioned thoughts. Don't try to cover them up. Stay with them and see the effect they are having on your behavior towards others. STOP and THINK before you react.

As soon as you notice false, fearful thinking, inhale for two seconds, exhale for four seconds. Let go and slow yourself down. Look for the truth. Then ask yourself the four questions in the "Intelligent Questioning" box in the previous chart to check whether your first thoughts and feelings are true or false. Then replace any wrong information with true information, such as in the following chart.

EXAMPLES OF FALSE THINKING	EXAMPLES OF TRUE INFORMATION
All blue-skinned people are dangerous.	All such broad statements are stereotypes based on conditioned thinking. Individuals are all different.
Foreign people are strange and frightening.	A foreign person is simply someone from another country. If I were in their country, I would be foreign.
I need to defend against "them."	There is only one group: "we humans."
"They" are a threat to my beliefs.	Beliefs can separate people. They probably feel threatened by my beliefs as well.
My country is much better than theirs.	We all share the same planet, Earth.
"They" make me uncomfortable, but I must learn to tolerate them.	If I learn to understand them, I will certainly feel more comfortable with them.
"They" have weird customs.	Every culture has different customs, and the customs of other cultures are always interesting.
"Their" clothes are strange.	Clothes are only costumes. They have nothing to do with the person inside.
"Their" language is odd.	Our language probably sounds odd to them. And wouldn't be fun to learn a few words of theirs?
"They" look and act different.	What a boring world it would be if everybody were the same.

When we're angry with someone we perceive as different and a threat, this anger comes from fear. Remember: We feel what we think. Understanding that our anger is hiding our fear, we have a choice. We can stay angry. Or we can uncover the fear and deal with it.

DISCOVERY 29
Anger hides fear. Understand the fear!

How do we recognize our fears? Our brains usually show these as thoughts that begin with "What if " and present frightening images, such as:

What if . . . they take over our school, town, country?
What if . . . they want to belong to our group?
What if . . . they take all the good jobs?
What if . . . they want us to believe in their ways?

Since we know that our thoughts affect our behavior, we should try to replace our fearful thoughts with more realistic thoughts, such as:

What if . . . they're no different than us?
What if . . . they have new and interesting ideas?
What if . . . they only want to be our friends?
What if . . . they just want to live their lives in peace?

These thoughts would tend to make us more open and friendly, don't you think? We must examine our thoughts to understand whether they are false or true and what effect they are having.

It all starts with a thought.
A thought creates a feeling.
The feeling creates your action.
It's up to you.
You can stop prejudice in your brain,
right at the start, when you are first aware of it.

Conditioning in Global Proportions

We must go beyond this book. Becoming free of prejudice is an ongoing process. We need to continue to observe, to question, to recognize prejudice in action and stop it in its tracks.

Do we run the risk of being influenced in the future, perhaps by another political leader who wants to control the world? Could another dictator grab our support and convince us of the necessity of hurting others to ensure our survival? Might another group of people be imprisoned or put to death by "ethnic cleansing" in concentration camps—all because someone believes that one race, or religion, or political system is superior to another? Could a certain group of people be enslaved again as they were in early America? The answer, I think we can agree is yes, unless we are constant and loyal in our guard against prejudice. We can guard against prejudice by:

Acknowledging that wrong actions based on prejudice happen
Questioning how they happen, and
Keeping aware of conditioned reactions of any kind.

We have seen that prejudice is something we do out of fear. By understanding its roots and the way we create prejudice with our thoughts, we can end the conflict. We can begin to make a right-side-up world that isn't a dream, a world in which we don't fear one another and where we all can respect and learn from our differences.

Rights and Responsibilities

The foundation of free countries of the world is democracy. In a democracy we're supposed to have certain rights and, with them, certain responsibilities. For example, one of our rights is freedom of speech. But with this right comes the responsibility to use speech in an intelligent, constructive way, for the betterment of all.

ASK YOURSELF
What happens when we use our right to freedom of speech irresponsibly?

We also have the right to be intelligently educated, meaning that we have the right to accurate information. Otherwise, how can we make intelligent decisions for our lives and be responsible for our actions?

ASK YOURSELF
Is the reason I sometimes feel incapable of making intelligent decisions that I'm not getting accurate information?

If prejudice is an "unfavorable opinion formed beforehand without knowing the truth," how can prejudiced thinking make us intelligent? If we are denied accurate information, how can we think and speak intelligently?

The basis of a democracy is clear and intelligent thinking, and the opportunity to act in ways that bring equality and peace to all humanity. If we live in a country that wants us to think in a fixed, conditioned way, then are we free to learn? Why would leaders want to control people's thoughts and actions? Are they afraid to let people make their own choices? Do governments sometimes fear that people thinking for themselves will criticize the government, reject it, replace it?

DISCOVERY 30
**If we're conditioned to think in a certain way,
we cannot make intelligent decisions.
We cannot see the truth or act upon it
when we have only one piece of a puzzle.**

To ensure that you are thinking and acting intelligently, use the following checklist to check yourself in any given situation:

A Checklist to Avoid Prejudice
Before starting, ask yourself (and think carefully before you answer):
Do I want to protect myself from the truth, or learn from it? If your answer is yes:

Question everything. Assume nothing.
Dismiss second-hand information. Gather accurate information.

Do not pre-judge. Observe and think for yourself.
Question questionable authority.
Examine your own thinking! Are you thinking for yourself,
or are your thoughts thinking for you?
Act based on accurate information.

Prejudice has caused much conflict, including many wars. It's a very serious thing. Grown beyond its roots, it's hard to stop. Once off and running, it can create a lot of pain and suffering.

Now, as students of prejudice, what are you going to do with what we've been talking about? Memorize it? Or will you observe your own brain, see the root of prejudice there, and end it before it goes any further?

You are the source of your freedom from prejudice! Thinking is what has created prejudice and the problems of prejudice. In-sight can help you avoid those prejudices.

**When you look at the roots of the tree of prejudice,
you are looking at yourself —
because you are the world and the world is you.**

**But don't worry.
Just stop, look, and listen.
All you need is inside you.**

**Acting out of intelligence, rather than prejudice,
is the highest form of action.**

IN-SIGHTS

★ In a right-side-up world, there would be no prejudice. Men, women, children, people of all colors and nationalities are all treated respectfully.

★ You have now advanced beyond being able only to imagine prejudice as a concept. Now you are able to perceive prejudice—to see it in action, right as it's happening

★ People who hate are unaware of their programming. They act as if their hatred is based on reality rather than imagined impressions inherited from their Forgotten Ancestors.

★ We use prejudice to protect ourselves, unaware that we are actually harming ourselves and others.

★ Wrong information can lead us down the Path to Conflict. Thoughts cannot hurt us; that's why we must stay with them and learn how we've been conditioned to think.

★ When we start down the Path to Conflict, we must imagine a big, red STOP sign in our minds to stop our conditioned thoughts.

★ In a democracy, we have the right to speak freely. But with this right comes the responsibility to use speech in an intelligent, constructive way, for the betterment of all.

★ We also have the right to be educated and to acquire accurate information so that we can make intelligent decisions about how to live and how to be responsible for our actions.

★ Prejudice is a conditioned belief. Thinking and acting out of intelligence, rather than prejudice, is the highest form of action.

THINKING FOR YOURSELF

✦ Do you see—at school, in your community, in the world—evidence of people being treated unequally?

✦ When we just look at such acts of prejudice honestly, do you recognize them as something you yourself might have done to someone?

✦ What do you think most makes the world "upside down?" A few people highly rewarded over the majority? Acting out of old tribal beliefs that separate the human race as a whole? Judging people by the color of their skin?

✦ Do you think that fighting can bring about peace?

✦ What do you think we mean when we say that our "vision is impaired"? Is it that we see what we've learned to believe rather than what "is"? What is "false self-talk"?

✦ Why do you think some people believe in "supremacy"? Do you think they are afraid of something?

✦ Do you think we hurt ourselves when we don't accept responsibility that belongs to us? How so?

✦ If I told you that "the food those people eat is strange," what true information would you present to replace this false thinking.

✦ When was the last time you felt hatred toward something or someone? Do you believe someone else caused you to hate, or do you believe you created it? Do you think it hurt you to feel hatred?

✦ What does it mean when we say that acting from intelligence, rather than prejudice, is the highest form of action?

✦ What does it mean to say that what we are comes from our thoughts, and that with our thoughts, we make the world?

List of Discoveries

Here is a handy list that you can use to review in your mind the Discoveries you have made through reading this book. I hope these will help keep a light shining for you that will allow you clearly see the roots of prejudice.

DISCOVERY 1
When you can observe clearly for yourself, you can stop prejudice.

DISCOVERY 2
**The best way to understand the meaning of prejudice
is to experience it firsthand.**

DISCOVERY 3
**In modern times, tribal groups and behavior can threaten the security
of our human race. Why? Because they separate people.**

DISCOVERY 4
**food + shelter = physical needs
sharing a way of life with others = psychological needs
physical needs + psychological needs = safety and security
A sense of safety and security comes
when both our physical and mental needs are satisfied.**

DISCOVERY 5
Fear creates conflict.

DISCOVERY 6
**Deeply ingrained in our brain cells, old tribal ways continue to
make us prisoners of the past.**

DISCOVERY 7
Our survival depends upon understanding we are all members of
one tribe—the Human Race.

DISCOVERY 8
You can change the world when you think for yourself.
A journey of a thousand miles begins with the first step.

DISCOVERY 9
Although prejudice may be something you encountered in the past, it
can continue, and make you unhappy in the present.

DISCOVERY 10
Prejudice is like a House of Mirrors.
All the images you have of others are created by you.

DISCOVERY 11
Prejudice causes our thinking to get "out of focus,"
making us judge what we see inaccurately.

DISCOVERY 12
Acting in prejudiced ways is not orderly or safe.
It is acting out of ignorance.

DISCOVERY 13
When we become prejudiced by not being aware,
we become numb to life around us. We accept the opinions of other people
without finding out the facts for ourselves.

DISCOVERY 14
There's only one enemy,
the one we create in our brain!

DISCOVERY 15
The "fight or flight" response is there for self-preservation.
It's an instinct to protect you from harm, which is a healthy and natural
response to real danger, but it can be activated unnecessarily by the
conditioned images we have of "the enemy."

DISCOVERY 16
Unaware of our programming, we act as if our hatred is necessary.
But we are the ones who are keeping it alive.

DISCOVERY 17
There are many authorities who can be of help to you throughout
your life. But it's important to be able to tell the difference between
authorities who have your best interests at heart and those who do not.

DISCOVERY 18
A problem created by prejudice is not "your" problem, "my" problem,
or even "our" problem. It is the problem, for it affects us all.

DISCOVERY 19
Prejudice ends when we can observe it in the making.
Once we observe it, we can stop it in ourselves.

DISCOVERY 20
Today, fighting to be the most powerful group
works against our security. It creates conflict between people
and keeps us from acting as a single race.

DISCOVERY 21
No one can be perfect. So trying to be perfect creates conflict.

DISCOVERY 22
The intelligent way to bring about good behavior is not through
judgment, but through intelligence.

DISCOVERY 23
Without prejudiced people, there can be no prejudice.

DISCOVERY 24
We believe what we've been either educated or
conditioned to believe. Education brings us understanding;
conditioning brings us prejudice.

DISCOVERY 25
Instead of fighting, we can reason with a bully.
We can use our brain instead of our fists.

DISCOVERY 26
No matter what level it gets to, prejudice needs to be stopped
in its tracks, before it rises to the next level.

DISCOVERY 27
No one else is to blame. I must take responsibility for my own life.

DISCOVERY 28
Prejudice is not something we're born with. It's something we learn.

DISCOVERY 29
Anger hides fear. Understand the fear!

DISCOVERY 30
If we're conditioned to think in a certain way, we cannot make
intelligent decisions. We cannot see the truth or act upon it when we
have only one piece of a puzzle.

THANK YOU

for taking this journey to discover the roots of prejudice. The only question left for you to answer is: "Where do I go from here?" You must continue on your own, and I wish you a good journey—free of the pain caused by prejudice.

P.S. I am delighted that the day I have finished this book—January 15—is Martin Luther King Day. Isn't that wonderful?

Remember— you can contact me directly with any questions at:

802-462-3900
Atrium@AtriumSoc.org

And please check out our web page at www.AtriumSoc.org

With care,

Terrence Webster-Doyle

INTERNATIONAL PRAISE FOR
DR. TERRENCE WEBSTER-DOYLE'S WORK

Why is Everybody Always Picking on Me? was cited by the *Omega New Age Directory* and one of the Ten Best Books of 1991, for its "atmosphere of universal benevolence and practical application."

> "These topics are excellent and highly relevant. If each of the major countries of the world were to have ten Drs. Webster-Doyle, world peace would be achieved over a period of just one generation."
> —Dr. Chas. Mercieca, Executive Vice-President,
> International Ass'n of Educators for World Peace,
> NGO, United Nations (ECOSOC), UNICEF & UNESCO

Acclaimed at the Soviet Peace Fund Conference in Moscow and published in Russia by Moscow's Library of Foreign Literature and Magister Publications.

> "Every publication from the pen of this author should make a signficant contribution to peace within and without. Highly recommended!"
> —*New Age Publishers and Retailers Trade Journal*

Dr. Webster-Doyle has been awarded the Robert Burns Medal for Literature by Austria's Albert Schweitzer Society, for "outstanding merit in the field of peace promotion."

> "Dr. Webster-Doyle takes the reader beyond the physical aspects of Karate training to a discovery of self. His books are an asset to parents, martial arts instructors, and students of all styles, ages, and rank levels."
> —Marilyn Fierro, 6th dan; Owner and Chief Instructor,
> Smithtown Karate Academy, Smithtown, N.Y.

Winner of Benjamin Franklin Awards for Excellence in Independent Publishing.

ABOUT THE AUTHOR

Dr. Terrence Webster-Doyle holds a Ph.D. in Health and Human Services as well as a sixth-degree black belt in Karate, and is co-founder and volunteer director of Martial Arts for Peace and the Atrium Society, a nonprofit organization. Dr. Webster-Doyle is a parent and former school teacher and administrator who has taught at the secondary, community college, and university level in psychology, education, and philosophy and served as a juvenile delinquency prevention task-force member.

Drawing on his diverse background and nearly forty years experience in peace education, Dr. Webster-Doyle developed his unique "How To Defeat the Bully Without Fighting Program" and has written seventeen books and eleven curricula in support of it. The program, which includes a book, curriculum, two videos, and a poster, is actively in use in hundreds of schools in the U.S. and around the world. The program focuses on his bestselling book, *Why Is Everybody Always Picking On Me?: A Guide to Handling Bullies,* which has helped thousands of young people worldwide to cope with the problem of bullying.

Dr. Webster-Doyle's internationally acclaimed Martial Arts for Peace and Education for Peace books have earned him the Benjamin Franklin Award for Excellence in Independent Publishing for six consecutive years. His books and programs have been endorsed by the National PTA, *Scouting Magazine* (for the Boy Scouts and Girl Scouts of America), National Education Association (NEA), Educators for Social Responsibility, the International Association of Educators for World Peace, and others. He was also awarded the prestigious Robert Burns Medal in literature by Austria's Albert Schweitzer Society for "outstanding merit in the field of peace promotion." A three-time Martial Arts Hall of Fame inductee, Dr. Webster-Doyle has been featured worldwide in the media, including a feature article in *Sports Illustrated for Kids.*

ABOUT THE ARTIST

Rod Cameron was born in 1948 in Chicago, Illinois, but has lived in southern California most of his life. He studied painting with "Dick and Jane" illustrator Keith Ward and at the Otis/Parson School of Design in Los Angeles. In 1985, Rod Cameron founded East/West Arts, Inc., a design and art studio in Ventura, California. His work has been shown on major network television and has received awards for its illustrative excellence.

ABOUT THE ATRIUM SOCIETY

The Atrium Society is a non-profit, non-sectarian, non-political organization whose goal is to bring to the general public an awareness of the role of psychological conditioning, including prejudice of all types, in creating conflict, and the dire need for conflict education programs for young people. Its International Youth Peace Literacy Book Donation Project raises funds to donate its educational materials to young people worldwide who need but cannot afford them. For further information about these worthwhile books and programs, contact the Atrium Society at 1-800-848-6021 or at www.AtriumSoc.Org.

BOOKS FOR YOUNG PEOPLE
BY DR. TERRANCE WEBSTER-DOYLE

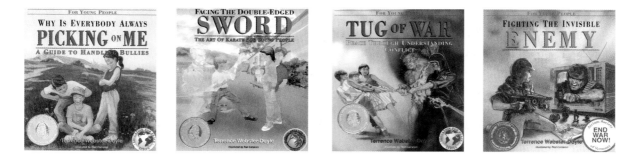

Why is Everybody Always Picking on Me? A Guide to Handling Bullies

A complete program for helping young people peacefully to avoid or resolve conflict, including stories, roleplaying, problem-solving, and other activities that teach both mental and physical self-defense skills. Includes a step-by-step program for dealing with bullies. Suitable for young people ages 8 through 18 and their parents.

8 1/2 x 9 1/2; 144 pp; 21 full-color illustrations; ISBN 0–8348–0467–0; $14.95 (soft)

Facing the Double-Edged Sword: The Art of Karate for Young People

A book for young people interested in finding non-violent solutions to conflict, teaching the true spirit of the martial arts through exciting stories about Karate and great Karate Masters. Also designed to help parents, teachers, and counselors seeking ways to teach young people healthy and humane ways to cope with conflict. Suitable for young people ages 8 through 18 and their parents

8 1/2 x 9 1/2; 96 pp; 21 full-color illustrations; ISBN 0–8348–0465–4; $14.95 (soft)

Tug of War: Peace Through Understanding Conflict

For young people concerned about violence and war, this book is filled with creative stories and activities showing how to resolve conflict in peaceful ways. It leads readers to discover the roots of violence, how we all create the "enemy," and how to deal with the consequences of our fears. Suitable for young people ages 8 through 18 and their parents.

8 1/2 x 9 1/2; 112 pp; 21 full-color illustrations; ISBN 0–942941-20-9; $12.95 (soft)

Fighting the Invisible Enemy: Understanding the Effects of Conditioning

For young people concerned with violence and its consequences, this book explores what conditoning is, how war can actually be created by the way we think about the world, and how .to deal with the consequences of our conditioning. Suitable for young people ages 8 through 18 and their parents.

8 1/2 x 9 1/2; 176 pp; 21 full-color illustrations; ISBN 0–942941-18-7; $12.95 (soft)

The "weathermark" identifies this book as a production of Weatherhill, Inc., publishers of fine books on Asia and the Pacific. Cover and illustrations: Rod Cameron. Book and cover design: Liz Trovato. Editorial supervision: Ray Furse. Production supervision: Bill Rose. Oceanic Graphic Printing, China. The typefaces used are Baskerville and Agenda.